HOW FIRM A FOUNDATION
A survey of church architecture in rural Georgia

By
Richard A. Noegel

Photographs by
Carol J. Mohor

Vilnius Press LLC
152 Court Street
Suite 2E
Portsmouth, NH 03801
www-vilnius-press.com

All rights reserved © 2014 by Richard Noegel

No part of this book may be reproduced or transmitted in any form or by any means, graphic, electronic, or mechanical, including photocopying, recording, taping, or by any information storage retrieval system, without the written permission of the publisher.

For information address:

Vilnius Press LLC
152 Court Street
Suite 2E
Portsmouth, NH 03801
www.vilnius-press.com

Did you know that...

...the "Cajuns" sojourned in Georgia at public expense before they finally migrated to Louisiana to settle?

...Georgia's earliest Baptist minister, Daniel Marshall, was arrested, tried, and sentenced to banishment in 1772—merely for preaching in the officially Anglican colony?

...John Wesley was brought up on charges before the Grand Jury in Savannah six times in 18 months—and that he ultimately fled from Georgia in the dead of night, never to return?

...the beloved "Father of Georgia," General Sir James Edward Oglethorpe, bart., was tried for treason by a British court martial for his conduct during the Jacobite uprising in 1745?

...the royal charter of the Georgia colony outlawed Roman Catholics, liquor, slavery, and lawyers—but that Jews were welcomed with open arms?

...the oldest public building in Georgia is a Lutheran church?

...Spanish monks introduced the first peach trees into Georgia and the first orange trees into Florida—in the 16th century?

"How firm a foundation,
Ye saints of the Lord,
Is laid for your faith
In His excellent Word!"
—from an 18th-century English hymn

Dedication

To all Georgians everywhere.

To those who came before me, especially my parents, without whose unstinting support this book would never have been completed.

To those who come after me, especially my children and grandchildren, without whom this book could have no meaning.

And to the memory of Sharon (2000); Brannen (2001); Frederick (2002); and Raymond (2013).

Deo Optimo Maximo

Acknowledgements

Special thanks to Carol for her willingness; for her unfailing good humor; for her photography; and for being the World's Best Traveling Companion. What fun it all was!

Special thanks to my sister Julie and to my dear friends Robert and Karen for their invaluable help in digitizing the manuscript. "Friends in need are friends indeed."

INTRODUCTION
Religion and the Founding and Settlement of Georgia

Spanish missions in Guale

In 1565, Spain established Saint Augustine, Florida, the first European colony to survive in what is now the United States. The following year, a party of Spanish soldiers from Saint Augustine became the first European inhabitants of what is now Georgia when they established outposts on the islands of Santa Catalina (now Saint Catherine's) and San Pedro (now Cumberland). Very soon after that, they established presidios and brought Jesuit priests to establish missions in Guale, which was their name for what is now coastal Georgia. Franciscan friars succeeded the Jesuits, and the missions that ultimately dotted the coast became outposts of Spanish civilization and power for a hundred years afterwards. Indeed, their influence persists even to the present day, as it was these Spanish monks who introduced the first peach trees into Georgia and the first orange trees into Florida. The history of ecclesiastical architecture in Georgia thus began during that period, although none of those early Spanish church buildings has survived to the present day. These Spanish colonial missions were in any event not the imposing edifices that would later be built in California, Texas, New Mexico, and elsewhere—the missions that are rightly so well known and so highly treasured today. The missions in Georgia came far earlier and were more primitive architecturally. According to Professor Spalding (see Reading List), they were wattle-and-daub huts that were roofed with palmetto fronds. However, the main Spanish mission, which was on San Pedro (now Cumberland Island), was rebuilt using iron nails and wood, with shingles for the roof, after having been destroyed by a storm in 1597. The Spanish missionaries enjoyed such great success in converting the Indians that in 1606, Archbishop Altamirano came to Guale (Georgia) from Cuba to confirm three thousand Native converts in the Roman Catholic faith.

England lays claim to Guale

England first laid claim to what is now Georgia in 1663 when King Charles II granted an immense tract of land to eight of his faithful supporters—the Lords Proprietors of the Carolina Colony. That land grant extended from 36°N latitude (Albemarle Sound) southward to 31°N latitude. Two years later, the king extended the grant southward to 29°N latitude, which included even Saint Augustine! But actual occupation and control of Guale (coastal Georgia) remained with the Spaniards until 1686, when they were finally forced to quit the area, owing to pressure from pirates and Indians and from the English, who by then were established in Carolina. In 1763, Spain was finally obliged to abandon even Florida to Britain. Spain regained possession of Florida in 1783 at the end of the American Revolution but finally ceded it to the United States in 1819.

British Crown charters "the colony of Georgia in America"

The Georgia colony came into formal, legal existence in June of 1732 when King George II granted a charter to a corporation, or "trust," whose members were to establish English settlements west and south of the Savannah and the Altamaha rivers. The royal charter stipulated that the Trustees, as the members of the corporation were collectively known, were to surrender the charter to the Crown, and thus to Imperial control (through the Board of Trade), after a period of twenty-one years. Until that time, the Trustees would be the proprietors of the colony, subject to royal authority and certain restrictions, and would direct all aspects of day-to-day operations in Georgia.

The Father of Georgia

General Sir James Edward Oglethorpe, son and heir of Sir Theophilus Oglethorpe, baronet, of Westbrook Place, at Godalming, Surrey, was born in London, probably in 1696. He was the only one of the Trustees ever to come to Georgia personally, and he is revered today as "the Father of Georgia." He was so well loved by the earliest settlers in Georgia that they called him "father," and they wept publicly when he had to return to England temporarily about 18 months after their arrival in Georgia. He would later be described by one of the Lutheran clergy in Georgia as "an excellent and blessed instrument of God."

When Oglethorpe was a young man, about 20 years before the beginning of the Georgia enterprise, his mother, Lady Oglethorpe, an ardent supporter of the Jacobite cause, enrolled him in Oxford University, which was a stronghold of Jacobite sympathy, but within the year, he forsook Oxford and went to St.-Germain, France (near Paris), to live with his mother and his two sisters, all of whom were attached to the court of the exiled King James III & VIII (James Francis Edward, the "Old Pretender"). (The Jacobites were partisans of the Stuart dynasty, which, in the person of the Old Pretender's father, King James II & VII, had been driven from the British throne by William and Mary in the "Glorious Revolution" of 1688, discussed later in this Introduction.) But although Oglethorpe adored his mother—a remarkable, even redoubtable woman—life as a member of the Stuart court-in-exile was not for him. After he had been only a very short time in France, his mother's kinsman, the Duke of Argyle, secured a post for him as an officer on the staff of Prince Eugène of Savoy, a brilliant military commander with whom young Oglethorpe saw combat during the siege of Belgrade. He immediately distinguished himself in the prince's service, possessed as he was of an adventuresome spirit that would later also lead him to give up the life of an English baronet to sojourn in the wilds of 18th-century Georgia and establish the colony on a sure footing.

Oglethorpe was elected to Parliament in 1722 and served until 1754. It was during his early service in Parliament that he was appointed to a committee whose task was to inspect and report on conditions in several English prisons. The committee had been appointed at Oglethorpe's behest after he saw the ghastly prison conditions of the time when visiting one of his friends who had been imprisoned for debt. In January 1732, Oglethorpe made a speech in the Commons to call for British assistance to the persecuted Protestants of Europe, particularly the Moravians. Oglethorpe also was a member of the Society for the Propagation of the Gospel in Foreign Parts and a member of a council that looked after the welfare of orphans. He interested himself also in relieving the poor and in defending seamen against impressment.

The Trustees counted both Anglicans and Dissenters among their number, but Oglethorpe and the Viscount Perceval (later the Earl of Egmont) and some of the other Trustees insisted that the Church of England occupy a privileged position in Georgia. That will be discussed presently.

Purpose of the colony

The belief that Georgia was founded for the relief and resettlement of inmates of British debtors' prisons romanticizes the truth somewhat. That motive, although important, was only one of several. Britain established Georgia as, first and foremost, a military buffer between her own Carolina colony and Spanish Florida, and also to further the mercantilist policies of the British government and to provide a refuge for the unfortunate of Britain and for persecuted Protestants in Europe. Without these commercial, politico-religious, and military considerations, the level of support for the Georgia enterprise—particularly military and financial support—would probably have been much lower, assuming that there would have been any at all. It must be remembered that Oglethorpe was a brigadier general in the British army and that, in those days, politics and religion were one and the same thing.

It is true that hundreds of poor and unemployed persons applied to colonize Georgia but, although there were debtors among them, none of the colony's backers or promoters ever visited British prisons to select debtors for resettlement in Georgia. Such had indeed been the hope of the Rev. Dr. Thomas Bray—Anglican clergyman; friend of Oglethorpe; one of the founders of the Society for the Propagation of the Gospel in Foreign Parts; and one of Britain's leading humanitarians—but he died before any such action could be taken. The Trustees personally investigated every settler who was to set sail for Georgia at the Trustees' expense—probably the most meticulous screening process for settlers in any colony in British America. Unfortunate but worthy persons predominated among those selected to begin life anew in Georgia. The persons who were to pay for their own passage were investigated along with any servants they brought to Georgia. Apparently no one was accepted merely because he had been imprisoned for debt. The idea that Georgia was established first and foremost as a haven for those languishing in British debtors' prisons, although suitably romantic, is not accurate. As Professor Coleman has written (see Reading List), no more than a dozen former inmates of any sort of debtors' prisons were ever sent to Georgia for a new chance in life. And even then, most such persons who were sent showed themselves as incapable of running their lives in Georgia as they had been in Britain. Actual British settlement of "the colony of Georgia in America" began with the arrival of the first settlers in February 1733 aboard the ship *Anne*.

Church of England transplanted

Georgia was founded and settled during the great Age of Enlightenment, during which time there was a great deal of humanitarian activity, and, as well might be expected, organized religion played a major role in the establishment of the colony. Georgia became a favorite charity of many persons in Britain and Ireland in the 1730s, and the Church of England repeatedly sent missionaries to Georgia during the early days, although, with the notable exceptions of Whitefield and Zouberbuehler, they did not manage to accomplish much that was of an enduring quality. The massive publicity campaign to generate support for the Georgia colony caught the fancy of the British nation, and the name of James Oglethorpe became a household word in the Britain of the mid-eighteenth century.

Bibles and religious tracts were sent from Britain and Ireland. Indeed, more than one hundred clergymen and churches (in Britain) received, at their own request, commissions to collect money for the support of the Georgia enterprise. The Archbishop of Canterbury and many bishops, archdeacons, deans, chapters, and collegiate and parochial clergy made generous contributions to the great and widely admired enterprise. Stevens (see Reading List) quotes the Trustees' journal as showing that when the *Anne* arrived with the first settlers, she carried also "115 Bibles and Testaments, 116 Common Prayerbooks, 72 Psalters, 312 Catechisms, 56 Bishop Gibson's *Family Devotions*, and 437 other religious volumes." Stevens tells us also that during the first two years of British settlement of Georgia, supporters in Britain and Ireland donated "over 2600 Bibles, Testaments, and religious books...." Within two years of the original settlers' arrival, a Parish Library was established in Savannah.

Importance of the Great Awakening

Moreover, the Great Awakening was gaining tremendous momentum just at the time the Georgia colony was erected. The Great Awakening was a series of religious revivals that began in Puritan New England about 1725 and swept through the whole of British America for about the next 50 years, indelibly stamping American life and culture with its religious and emotional fervor. The movement for American rights and independence would have been almost inconceivable apart from the general climate engendered by the Great Awakening, the effects of which remain with us to this day. It was during this same period that the Methodist movement began in England and that the Wesleys and their friend George Whitefield labored in Georgia.

Religious latitude in colonial Georgia

Permanent English settlement of Georgia began in February 1733, with the arrival in the estuary of the Savannah River of Oglethorpe and the original colonists, most of whom were, of course, Anglicans (Episcopalians). The leading organized religious groups in colonial Georgia were the Anglicans, Lutherans, Jews, Congregationalists, and Quakers. Roman Catholics, or "papists," as the royal charter referred to them, were prohibited, and although there were more than a few Baptists, they had no organized congregation until 1772—the very eve of the Revolution and independence. In general, the official exclusion of Catholics from colonial Georgia was apparently not strictly enforced. French settlements to the west (Mobile, New Orleans, and others) and Spanish settlements to the south (St. Augustine, Pensacola, and others) made it a military necessity for the British that Georgia remain firmly in Protestant hands, but public and private records show that there were Catholics living in Georgia and taking an equal place with their Protestant and Jewish neighbors in the commercial and even in the judicial affairs of the colony. For example, during his brief and turbulent sojourn in Georgia, John Wesley was hauled up before the local magistrates in Savannah at least six times on various charges. There is no doubt that the charges might have had, perhaps, some kernel of truth in them, but, even so, his accusers seem to have been the trouble-making sort in the first place. In any event, the record of one of these proceedings, in 1737 (on an array of charges that amounted to accusing him of being, in modern parlance, a "closet Catholic" as well as a general nuisance), shows that Catholics and Baptists were living in Georgia and taking full part in colonial life, because Wesley objected to the composition of his jury, which included, in his words, "a Frenchman, a papist, an infidel, and three Baptists."

The number of Roman Catholics was certainly very, very small, and getting a priest could not even be considered, so there was no organized Catholic congregation in pre-Revolutionary Georgia. It is probably because they were so few in number that they were integrated easily into the life of the officially Protestant colony.

The "Cajuns" sojourn in Georgia

It seems that the only time Catholics were actually refused permission to settle in colonial Georgia was in 1755, when several hundred Catholics—the Acadians—having been expelled by the British from Canada, arrived in Georgia seeking a refuge and a home. They were permitted to remain in Georgia for the winter; indeed, they were sheltered at public expense. But when spring came, they were expelled from the colony. Eventually, of course, they would settle in southern Louisiana, where their descendants are well-known today as the "Cajuns" (i.e., the Acadians). All in all, however, the atmosphere in Georgia was more tolerant in the sphere of religion than in probably any other colony. The only real sign of religious persecution in colonial Georgia was the arrest and trial of the Baptist minister Daniel Marshall–and that action was not supported by the existence of any law but probably resulted, as, perhaps, in the case of John Wesley, from personal enmity. Daniel Marshall was sentenced to banishment, but the sentence was not enforced.

Earliest efforts of the English Church

Well before the first settlers embarked from England, the Trustees had decided that the Church of England would occupy a privileged position in Georgia. So it was that when Oglethorpe and the first settlers arrived, Christ Church had already been established as the official church for the town of Savannah, making it today Georgia's oldest Christian congregation. After the Crown chartered Georgia in June 1732, the Common Council of the Trustees met on November 8, 1732, and instructed Oglethorpe to "set out three hundred acres of land in Georgia in America to be appropriated for the use of the Church of the town of Savannah, and a site for the Church, and the minister's house in the town and likewise a burial place at a proper distance from the town." On the same day, the Rev. Dr. Henry Herbert, son of Lord Herbert of Cherbury, offered to go to Georgia to perform "all religious and ecclesiastical offices" at his own expense, free of charge to the colonists or the Trustees. The Trustees accepted his offer instantly, and Dr. Herbert thus became Georgia's first clergyman. His appointment for service in Georgia was for a one-year term. It lasted only a matter of weeks, however, for Dr. Herbert fell ill shortly after his arrival and accordingly embarked upon a return voyage to England, during which he died. According to McCain (see Reading List), Dr. Herbert's career can be taken as a metaphor for practically everything undertaken by the English Church during the first 20 years of the colony. General Oglethorpe, Dr. Bray, the Viscount

Perceval, Lord Shaftesbury, and the other Trustees were motivated, as were the colony's many Anglican supporters throughout Britain and Ireland, by the highest hopes and noblest ideals. The same high purposes motivated the Trustees' every action in trying to carry out their overall plan. But while the Trustees were governing the colony, their sincere efforts at religious instruction and church-building were hampered by the indifference of a great many settlers; by the oft-fractious quarrels between civil magistrates and duly appointed clergy, and between the clergy and their vocal and sometimes vicious civilian detractors; and by the great diversity in religious opinion of the English-speaking population. The colony suffered, moreover, from the generally ineffectual (and sometimes downright damaging) efforts of nearly all the Anglican missionaries who served in Georgia.

During the colonial period, the Lutherans and the Quakers were noteworthy exceptions. And by the end of the Revolution, the Baptists had assumed a clear dominance of religion in Georgia, with the Methodists firmly in second place and growing by leaps and bounds by the end of the 18th century. It should be remembered, though, that a great many of the settlers in pre-Revolutionary Georgia, if not actually the majority of them, did not belong to any church at all, whether from indifference or from a lack of opportunity is both unknown and unknowable. However, the writings of a couple of contemporary clergymen may shed some light on that situation. The Rev. Mr. Samuel Quincy, Rector of Savannah, and a relation of the Massachusetts Quincys, wrote to authorities in London in 1735 that "religion seems to be the least minded of anything in Georgia." In 1746, the Rev. Mr. Bartholomew Zouberbuehler wrote that the people seemed "in general religiously disposed," but by 1760, the Rev. Mr. Zubly of Savannah's Independent Presbyterian Church, wrote that religion was at a low ebb everywhere in Georgia.

Irish Protestants settle in Georgia

When the eighteenth-century British rulers of Ireland extended their wholesale persecution of Catholics to include non-Anglican Protestants as well, huge numbers of Irish Protestants—some Norman-Irish and some Scotch-Irish—migrated to America and settled in Georgia and elsewhere. These Irish in colonial Georgia were almost entirely Presbyterian. Large numbers of them settled, beginning in 1768, along the Ogeechee River in Saint George's Parish (now, roughly, Burke and Jefferson counties), where they prospered and flourished (see Reading List). Many of them immediately became ardent supporters of American independence. Soon afterwards, these Irish Presbyterians were joined by their French co-religionists, the Huguenots. The descendants of these French and Irish settlers populate that part of eastern Georgia today. Ebenezer Presbyterian Church near Louisville (Jefferson County) and Bethel Presbyterian Church at Vidette (Burke County) are the two old Irish Presbyterian congregations of that vicinity; they continue to function in our own time. Both congregations sprang from an earlier Irish Presbyterian congregation that met at Fleeting's Meeting House in Queensborough (now Louisville), but contention over the question of American independence brought about a split in the congregation, and the members formed Ebenezer (patriots) and Bethel (tories).

Scottish Highlanders settle in Georgia

The Irishmen of Saint George's Parish were not, however, the only Presbyterians in Georgia, nor even the first ones. In 1735, a group of Scottish Highlanders had settled on the banks of the Altamaha River, which at that time was Georgia's southern frontier. They called the district Darien, and they named their town New Inverness, but eventually the town came to be called Darien, the name by which we know it today. These hardy, energetic settlers were quite well-suited to military service, and it was they who, under the command of a Captain McKay and a Lieutenant Sutherland, defeated the Spaniards so decisively at Bloody Marsh in July of 1742 that Georgia would remain "permanently" in British hands, safe at last from further threat of encroachments by the Spaniards in Florida and Cuba. (Oglethorpe was technically in command of the British forces at Bloody Marsh, although he happened to be a short distance away from the actual combat when it came about. Nevertheless, credit for Britain's repulse of Spain's invasion of Georgia went to Oglethorpe, and the British victory at Bloody Marsh made him the most famous and popular figure in England—for a time.) Furthermore, through their thriftiness and hard work, these Highland Scots played a major role in laying the foundations of economic stability and prosperity in colonial Georgia. Their efforts at establishing a regular congregation and at constructing a church building were significant. Their minister, the Rev. Mr. John McLeod, scion of a branch of the Dunnegan family (McLeod of McLeod), had received an excellent recommendation from his fellow clergymen in Scotland, and he had sustained a good examination before the Presbetery of Edinburgh preceding his ordination and commission in October 1735. He was appointed, as Stevens tells us (see Reading List), by the directors of the Scottish branch of the Society for the Promotion of Christian Knowledge, "not only to officiate as minister of the Gospel to the Highland families going [to Georgia]," but also to endeavor to convert the local Indians. Their church building, built before 1750 and known as "the Old Meeting House," was erected with Oglethorpe's support and assistance and with the understanding that it would serve only until the Darien Scots could fund construction of a proper church building. (Mr. McLeod had learned that a lady in London had left, according to Stevens, a "disputable sum of several hundred pounds upon the East India Company, to be applied to the use of the Presbyterian Church in Georgia.") After a sojourn in the Darien district of about five or six years, the Rev. Mr. McLeod resettled on Edisto Island, South Carolina.

Other Presbyterians

The Presbyterians of Savannah organized that city's Independent Presbyterian Church in 1755, and by 1758 they had constructed a brick church building facing Ellis Square, but it no longer stands. The term "independent" is to be interpreted quite literally, for the Church of Scotland (Presbyterian) had no hand in organizing the congregation, and the church was not subject to any ecclesiastical authority outside of its own local membership. Their present building in downtown Savannah, although outside the scope of this work, is without doubt one of the finest church buildings in America. The ministry of J. J. Zubly, who became the congregation's minister in 1760, is one of the bright spots in colonial Georgia's ecclesiastical history. Mr. Zubly was a Swiss and was ordained to the sacred ministry at the German Church in London, so some scholars think it possible that he was not technically a Presbyterian. But as a Swiss, it is not unlikely that he was a Calvinist. Also, he required converts to embrace The Westminster Confession of Faith in order to become members of his Savannah flock. And, most convincing of all, when the settlers at Vernonsburg and adjacent villages had petitioned the Trustees in February 1743 to send them "a minister of Calvinistical principles," they had specified Zubly by name, so he is counted as one of Georgia's early Presbyterian clergymen. Zubly, along with the Rev. Mr. John Osgood, who served the Congregationalists at Midway (Liberty County), were the most noteworthy Presbyterian clergymen of pre-Revolutionary Georgia.

The first ordination of a Presbyterian clergyman in Georgia would take place after the Revolution and far in the back-country, in what is now Washington (Wilkes County). There, in 1790, John Springer was ordained and was charged with the care of three Wilkes County congregations. The ceremony took place in the open air beneath a large poplar tree, which ever after was called "the Presbyterian Poplar." It lived for more than 150 years after the ordination ceremony, and when it died naturally, it was felled, and its wood was used to make the chancel Cross and the offering plates that are still in use in the Washington Presbyterian Church to this day.

As mentioned earlier, another group of Presbyterians—and an incalculably important one—was the Huguenots, who had been obliged to emigrate from France because of persecution. They settled largely in South Carolina, Virginia, and Georgia, where their many descendants still live. Charleston, South Carolina, still has a Huguenot Church today.

The Moravians and the Quakers

As well, there were small communities of Moravians and Quakers in colonial Georgia. The Moravians arrived in 1735, but they had come to Georgia with the express understanding that they were to be absolutely exempt from military service. Frontier life in a military buffer colony was, however, no place for religious pacifists. Their opposition to war, even in self-defense, was incomprehensible to the other colonists, and there was also internal dissension in their community and a good deal of tension between them and the Salzburg Lutherans, so the Moravians left Georgia for Pennsylvania. During their stay in Georgia, however, they wielded enormous influence over John Wesley, who—fortunately—relied entirely on their counsel during his frequent troubles. Today, there is once again a Moravian congregation in Georgia, although it is not, in fact, by any means the "first" Moravian church in Georgia.

The Quaker settlement, called Wrightsborough, was in the back-country, in what is now McDuffie County. The Quakers came to Georgia from North Carolina about 1770, after the lands to the west of Augusta were ceded to Georgia by the Creek Nation. As one might rightly expect from a settlement of Quakers, Wrightsborough was prosperous and orderly, and probably numbered about 600 souls at the height of its development. Some of the Quakers owned slaves even though their religious discipline forbade the practice. But Quaker slaveholders knew that to free their slaves would be to place them into the hands of slave-traders, since outright manumission was not possible under the law. Accordingly, they resolved to keep their slaves until the day that slavery should come to an end and to treat them with kindness in the interim. They also entered into a covenant with one another not to trade in slaves except among themselves only. But the invention of the cotton gin in 1793 made large-scale cotton planting profitable, which increased the need for slaves, so the Wrightsborough community broke up, and most (but not all) of Georgia's Quakers emigrated from Georgia and settled in Miami County, Ohio. The others kept their slaves, remained in Georgia, and became Baptists.

Support for the colonial clergy

None of the clergy of colonial Georgia received a large salary. The usual sum paid by the missionary societies was £50 per annum. They required that this be supplemented in some way, so the Trustees usually furnished ministers with a house, a glebe of 300 acres, and one or two assorted servants or farm hands. The missionary societies and the Trustees granted financial support to the Salzburgers (Lutherans) and to the Presbyterians as well as to the Anglicans. The king and other authorities usually assisted each new mission of the Anglican Church in small ways. After 1758, the Anglican Church became, by law, the Established Church in Georgia.

Earliest church buildings in British Georgia

Few church buildings were erected in Georgia during the first two decades of the colonial period. Numerous persons were interested in building a Parish Church for Savannah (Christ Church), and money was collected for that purpose for several years after the initial settlement, but construction was repeatedly delayed. The first building used for church services in Savannah was a sort of cabin of rough boards, which was constructed at the Trustees' expense in 1735. It was 12 feet wide and 36 feet long. But when a court house was later erected in Savannah, it was used also for public worship. It was in the court house that John Wesley held services during his short and very troubled sojourn in Georgia. John Wesley was proficient in Hebrew, Arabic, French, Spanish, Italian, and German, and, while in Savannah, he frequently held services on Sundays in English, French, German, and Italian. (There was a small group of Italian Piedmontese whose task was to teach the other colonists to produce silk, Georgia's first cash crop, hence the mulberry leaf and silkworm on the first Great Seal of the infant colony. Queen

Caroline, wife of George II, the king for whom Georgia is named, had a dress made of Georgia silk.)

Between 1735 and 1738, a good deal of money was raised for building a church (Anglican), and in 1737, some materials were sent from England to begin construction, but that was the extent of operations at that time. It was not until 1744 that work on the Savannah Parish Church (Christ Church) actually began, more than 11 years after the arrival of the first settlers. But only the roof, floor, and framework were finished before the money ran out, and construction came to a halt in the summer of 1745 (there was turbulence in Britain at the time). Nothing more was done until the spring of 1747, when the Salzburgers were asked to produce sufficient lumber from their sawmill to finish the job. Bolzius, the Salzburgers' pastor as well as their civic leader, said that they would gladly do so but that in his judgment the existing structure had become too rotten to go ahead with any further construction. But go ahead it did, with more or fewer interruptions, until it was ready for dedication on July 7, 1750.

The consecration of the new church, so long desired and needed, was a notable event in the life of the colony. The church itself was large and handsome, at least in comparison with other buildings in Georgia in 1750. The foundations were of real stone, and the outside of the building was finished with cement that was set off with lines to give the appearance of stone; the interior was of white plaster. Its windows were glazed with English glass that had been imported especially for the purpose. Cost over-runs were a problem: expenses ran approximately double the original estimates. Even then, the Trustees had to contribute £100 of their own money to make final preparations for permanently occupying the building. It remained the finest church building in Georgia until the Salzburgers finished re-building Jerusalem Lutheran Church at New Ebenezer (present-day Effingham County) in 1769.

A small "chapel" was built at Frederica (Saint Simon's Island) as early as 1739. It was 60 feet long and 20 feet wide. Employees of the

Trustees cut most of the wood and milled it for lumber, and they did most of the construction work as well, so that the cost was comparatively low—about £50. In Augusta, "a handsome church" had been erected by 1750 at the expense of private citizens as one of several inducements for the Trustees to secure an Anglican missionary for the town, but it was really not much more than an inexpensive chapel, despite its promoters' descriptions. The Trustees provided the Augusta church with "some purple cloth for the Pulpit and Communion Table, a Silver Cup and Patin...and some Glass windows." This was the beginning of St. Paul's Episcopal Church, still thriving today in downtown Augusta.

"Bound for the Promised Land"

After the arrival of Oglethorpe and the original band of settlers in 1733, no other settlers were expected right away. But a chain of events that had begun long before and far away was to produce the unexpected arrival of a group of about 45 new settlers in July, before the English settlement in Georgia was even six months old. The group's arrival was unexpected because it was unauthorized. But these new settlers had paid their own passage and had therefore been able to act without the knowledge or permission of the Trustees. These new arrivals were Jews, hoping to find the liberty in Georgia that had for centuries been denied them in Europe and Britain. King Edward I ("Longshanks") had expelled the Jews from England in 1290, and until Oliver Cromwell lifted the ban against them in 1655, Jews were forbidden by Edward's royal decree to live in England. The Jewish colonists in Georgia were, however, not English, but Portuguese and German Jews who had lived in England for only a comparatively short time.

When they arrived in Georgia, they found the colony threatened with complete disaster in the form of an epidemic of fever that had already killed more than 10% of the small population—including the colony's only physician. But one of the Jews was a Dr. Nuñes, who had been personal physician to the Grand Inquisitor of Portugal, and his specialty was, happily, infectious diseases. According to Oglethorpe's report to the Trustees, Dr. Nuñes stopped the epidemic in its tracks so that "no one died afterwards." Disaster was thus averted. Jews, unlike Roman Catholics, had not been specifically excluded from settling in Georgia, so Oglethorpe not only allowed them to stay, but granted them all rights and privileges granted to other settlers, and required of them all responsibilities required of other settlers, including the right to bear arms; the duty to serve in the militia; the right to own property; and the liberty to practice their religion. These arrangements were far more accommodating than those enjoyed (or endured) by Jews at various times in New Amsterdam (New York) and New England, where both Dutch and English authorities and civilians subjected them, and had subjected them, to various indignities and restrictions.

In England, the Trustees were dismayed at the turn of events in Georgia, and they sought to have Oglethorpe expel the Jews from the colony, but he refused and they stayed. They became completely integrated into all facets of life in Savannah — except among themselves. The German Jews were more strictly observant than were the Portuguese and Spanish Jews, who, after all, had been forced for two centuries to live outwardly as Catholics. These differences were the source of continuing friction between the two Jewish groups. They maintained separate congregations for a time, but their internal divisions did not give occasion for any pubic offense, and these early Jewish settlers were respected citizens from the start, just as their many descendants in Georgia are to this day.

Although there was a bit of friction between the Portuguese and German Jewish communities, there was a history of good will and charitable assistance between the German Jews and the Salzburgers, who settled in Georgia in 1734 at Oglethorpe's invitation.

"To Canaan's fair and happy land"

The Salzurgers were, as already mentioned, Lutherans who had been turned out of their homes, stripped of their possessions, and forced into exile by the Roman Catholic archbishop of Salzburg, Austria, where the Lutheran Reformation had made too much headway for the archbishop's comfort. After their expulsion from Austria, they sojourned for a time in Augsburg, Germany, and they wandered, homeless, throughout Germany and the Netherlands. Eventually, Oglethorpe invited them to settle in Georgia. Their congregation, Jerusalem Lutheran Church, was organized in 1733 during the Salzburgers' sojourn in Germany, making it Georgia's second-oldest Christian congregation. After settling in Georgia, they established an orphanage with the assistance of the Trustees, and at first they worshiped in the orphanage building.

The Salzburgers build. And build. And build.

In 1750, however, with their own hands they built their first church building—a well-built wooden structure in their town, Ebenezer. It was about that same time that construction of Christ Church was at long last completed in Savannah. Construction of both buildings used lumber from the Salzburgers' sawmill. Neither building stands today. The Salzburgers soon abandoned their town because the location was an unhealthful one. They re-established themselves a short distance away and built a new town on the very banks of the Savannah River in present-day Effingham County, which they called New Ebenezer. The Salzburgers continued to meet with such success in their religious and economic efforts that within a year, they had built another church, called Zion, several miles from New Ebenezer, for the use of those who lived on plantations rather than in the town. When success continued to crown success, the Salzburgers found it necessary in 1751—just a year later—to construct a third building, Bethany Lutheran Church. All three buildings were wooden structures, well constructed of lumber produced at the Salzburgers' own sawmill. The interiors of all three buildings were painted white, and the exteriors were treated with turpentine to prevent rot.

It was at New Ebenezer that the Salzburgers built the church that stands today as the oldest public building in Georgia. The present Jerusalem Lutheran Church building was completed in 1769 to replace the wooden structure of 1750, and it has been in continuous use by the congregation ever since. It is a remarkable brick building—easily the finest church building in colonial Georgia—and, like the earlier wooden church, was the work of the Salzburgers' own hands. They molded and burnt the bricks on site. The finger-marks of children are visible in some of the bricks, the result of the children having carried the undried bricks from their molds to the firing ovens. The original church-bells, the oldest in Georgia, are still in use today by a congregation made up largely of descendants of the original Salzburger settlers.

Jerusalem Church was the center of New Ebenezer. Today, only the handsome brick church, one house, and the cemetery remain of that once-thriving colonial town. But there is a fine museum within the grounds of the church, which interested persons may visit.

The Salzburgers largely kept to themselves owing to the language barrier, and their pastors—Bolzius, Rabenhorst, Gronau, Lembke, and Driesler—had great influence within the necessarily close-knit community. These industrious Germans and Austrians enjoyed better economic success than most early Georgia colonists did. They operated a school and an orphanage, enjoyed great success with their sawmill, and had moderate success in producing silk. They produced several important leaders during the colonial, Revolutionary, and early state periods, including Georgia's first post-independence governor, John Adam Treutlen, who was raised in the orphanage at New Ebenezer. But the Salzburgers' efforts in the field of religion outstripped even their worldly successes. Indeed, in pre-Revolutionary Georgia, the Lutherans outstripped all other faiths by far and away, at least in terms of growth, accomplishment, and organizational integrity and effectiveness. Religious conditions among them were above reproach. Their communities were peaceful, cohesive, and prosperous.

Success of the Salzburgers

There were some very good reasons for the remarkable success of the Lutheran settlements. First, their religious lives and activities were carefully planned for them by ecclesiastical authorities in Germany and by the Society for the Propagation of the Gospel in Foreign Parts (in England), and those authorities required the Salzburgers to submit regular reports so that advice could be sent from Germany and England. To a man, their pastors were good and honorable, and they were remarkable spiritual leaders. Also, Bolzius's ministry was continuous throughout the earliest decades of the colonial period. Both Gronau and Lembke ministered for long terms in Georgia, quite unlike the clergy of other religious communities. The Salzburgers were remarkably unified in their faith, and they did not have to contend with the divisions that are so often brought about by contention between rival religious factions and which plagued the English-speaking settlers of Georgia. And perhaps most important, they had been called upon quite recently to suffer much for their faith, so their principles were of immense and *practical* importance to them. Their sufferings and wanderings in Europe, the danger and difficulties of their trans-Atlantic voyage, and the exigencies of frontier life in a place where not only their faith but also their language required them to depend upon one another quite naturally forged of them an extremely cohesive community.

"We shall meet on that beautiful shore"

Although the Salzburgers generally kept to themselves, they nevertheless maintained excellent relations with the other settlers in Georgia, except for the Moravians. But their connection with another group of German-speaking settlers invites some examination. These other German-speakers were the Ashkenazic (German) Jews of Savannah. Indeed, Pastor Bolzius was a guest of the German Jews at one of their worship services in Savannah in 1737, and not for the first or only time: when he wrote to his ecclesiastical superiors in Germany about worshiping with the Jews in Savannah, he stated quite specifically that they were using the same ceremonies that he had witnessed in Berlin. Interestingly, Pastor Bolzius's visit to the synagogue in Berlin was not the only contact that the Salzburg Lutherans had had with the Jews of Germany even before any of them had left Europe for Georgia. After being expelled from Salzburg very shortly before King George II chartered the Georgia colony, the Lutherans, as already mentioned, sojourned as refugees in Germany and the Netherlands, wandering as exiles from place to place in search of a safe haven. Wherever they went, they were met by Jews bearing gifts and offering moral support. By contrast, the Roman Catholic population had been forbidden to give even a drink of water to the Lutheran "heretics." The Jews of Germany and the Netherlands drew water from their own wells to relieve the sufferings of the Salzburger refugees and to water their animals, and they gave them gifts of money whenever they could afford to do so. This happened in many places: in Frankfurt-am-Main, in Coburg, in Würzburg, and in Bamberg. The synagogue in Berlin collected cash for the Salzburgers and gave them more than two hundred yards of linen to make clothing. In the city of Kassel, the local Jewish population collected a phenomenal sum of money for the homeless Salzburgers and gave it to them with the explanation that the Salzburgers' condition reminded them of the exodus of the Israelites from Egypt and that they both pitied and admired the Salzburgers for the reasons that had brought on their suffering and exile. With this sort of shared past and with the enormously powerful bond of a common language, it is not surprising that the German-speaking Jews and Lutherans established warm relations in colonial Georgia. In this connection, it is interesting and perhaps instructive to note that, according to Rabbi Rubin (see Reading List), the first two synagogues constructed in Savannah were financed without the necessity of taking subscriptions within the Hebrew congregation because the city's Christian population contributed all the money that was necessary to pay all construction costs.

The colonial Jewish congregation, Mikve Israel, is the oldest Jewish congregation in the South, and it is the third-oldest on the North American continent, only two congregations being older: Shearith Israel in

New York City and the Touro congregation (Jeshuat Israel) in in Rhode Island. Their beautiful 19th-century synagogue stands today in downtown Savannah, an urban area, and therefore falls outside the scope of this book. For the present work, I have drawn liberally from *Third to None*, Rabbi Rubin's scholarly and readable book, to which I refer the reader.

"The hosts of sin are pressing hard"

Slavery was outlawed during the early colonial period, as were rum, Roman Catholics and, interestingly enough, lawyers. Ale, beer, and wine, being considered harmless, were permitted apart from the prohibition of rum. Anyway, rum soon began to find a place in Georgia in spite of the law. In the end, neither juries nor magistrates would punish anyone for possession or consumption of liquor, and the authorities were therefore obliged to abandon their policy of prohibition. And virtually all of the Germans and Highland Scots opposed slavery, as did Oglethorpe, even though it became a fact of life in Georgia after the ban against it was lifted in 1750. Ultimately, of course, lawyers established themselves and their profession in Georgia, and the Roman Catholic Church gained official toleration with the Revolutionary government's Constitution of 1777, although under even that constitution, Catholics were excluded from the state legislature. Georgia's first Roman Catholic congregation would not be organized until 1790, which will be discussed later in this Introduction.

THE LATER COLONIAL PERIOD, REVOLUTION, AND INDEPENDENCE

Congregationalists settle and build at Midway

The Trustees of the colony surrendered their charter to the Crown in 1752, one year before the charter would have expired automatically. That same year, a large group of New England Puritans settled in Georgia. They had come originally from Dorchester, Massachusetts, and they had spent several generations in the Dorchester district of South Carolina, whence they migrated to Georgia. Among their number were also some Huguenots and Scots. They settled in Saint John's Parish, where they established a town that they called Midway, possibly because it is midway between Darien, on the Altamaha River, and Savannah, on the Savannah River, or possibly because the area and one of the rivers in it were originally called Medway, after a river in England. In any case, they established Midway Church, retaining their Congregationalist polity and theology, and therefore Saint John's Parish naturally became the cradle of the independence movement in Georgia in the 1770s and a hotbed of radical and revolutionary activity. Two of Georgia's three signers of the Declaration of Independence were Midway Congregationalists: Dr. Lyman Hall and Mr. Button Gwinnett. About 1755, the Congregationalists had completed a log meeting house in which to worship. The British burned it during the Revolution, and the present building, completed in 1792, was erected to replace it. The present building is a plain clapboard building with shuttered windows, a front gable adorned with two circular windows, and a simple belfry. It is a remarkably handsome building of refined proportions and lines reminiscent of a New England Puritan meeting house. The interior typifies church architecture in the early South, with its slave galleries against the side and back walls that necessitate the double tiers of windows, seen also in Bethesda Baptist Church (Greene County) and elsewhere. The Congregationalists of Midway were served by Presbyterian ministers, most notably John Osgood.

During the invasion of Georgia in 1864, the Yankees, as the British before them, horrifically vandalized Midway Church.

Provincial Assembly establishes the Church of England in Georgia

By 1754, a royal government was in place in the new Royal Province of Georgia. The Church of England was made the lawfully Established Church of the province in 1758. Establishing the Anglican Church as the colony's official religion was not intended to outlaw other Protestant faiths, but merely to give it the privileged position it enjoyed in England and Ireland. There were powerful reasons for this.

First of all, George I, the Elector (king) of Hanover and a great-grandson of James I of England and VI of Scotland, had been called to the British throne from Germany because he was a Protestant and because his mother, Sophia, niece of the martyred King Charles I, was the granddaughter of King James I & VI. The purpose was to ensure that the Catholic Stuarts did not regain the British throne. There were many in Scotland, in Ireland, and in England (including the Oglethorpe family) who were known as "Jacobites" — partisans of the Stuart prince James Francis Edward, "the Old Pretender." Indeed, only about ten years after the initial settlement of Georgia, there was an armed Jacobite uprising in Britain, the purpose of which was to return the Stuarts to the British throne, but it ended disastrously for the Jacobites on Culloden Moor in 1746. (Incidentally, General Oglethorpe was court-martialed for treason because it was alleged that he was a "closet Jacobite" and that he had deliberately allowed the escape of the Jacobite army that he had defeated near Carlisle during the uprising. He was acquitted, but the reputation of England's most famous and popular man was ruined, and he became thereafter a social outcast. He was voted out of Parliament at the next election, which was held in 1754. He never returned to Georgia.) His extraordinary mother and his two sisters played intriguing roles as Jacobite sympathizers also. The sisters remained in France, both attaining the rank of marquise through advantageous marriages.

Second, the knowledge of what the return of a Catholic monarchy could mean was ever present. After all, it had been barely fifty years since King James II & VII, a Roman Catholic and the father of the Old Pretender, had prorogued Parliament when the members refused to go along with his appointment of Catholics to positions of command in the army.

Parliament did not convene again during his reign. James had also deposed the (Anglican) bishop of London and then foolishly chose only Catholics to witness the birth of his son and heir to his queen, Mary-Beatrice of Modena, giving rise to the Protestant partisans' (in)famous "warming-pan baby" allegations against James Francis Edward — James III & VIII, the Old Pretender.

In the end, the "Glorious Revolution" (1688) had forced James, the Old Pretender, to flee to France, abandoning the throne to his Protestant half-sister, Mary, and to her husband, Prince William of Orange.

Moreover, it had been only about eighteen months before the founding of Jamestown, Virginia, that the Catholic Guy Fawkes had tried, through the now-famous "Gunpowder Plot," to blow up the British Parliament building — with the members of Parliament inside. And besides, the name of Bloody Mary had not nearly been forgotten, and even the illiterate knew the horrific stories contained in *Foxe's Book of Martyrs*.

And third, there were Catholics to the south (Spanish Florida) and Catholics to the west of Georgia (Mobile, New Orleans, Ste.-Geneviève in present-day Missouri, and other French settlements along the Mississippi). Guarding against Catholic domination was a major part of many English policies during this period. Besides, in 1758, it so happened that Governor Ellis had it in mind to reconstitute Georgia's colonial assembly, according to Dr. Cashin (see Reading List). Establishment of the Church of England admirably suited Governor Ellis's purpose, so in 1758, he pushed through the colonial assembly — against the outspoken opposition of the Lutherans and Congregationalists, and against the tacit opposition of the Baptists and Presbyterians—a bill "for the Establishment of religious worship in the Province of Georgia and for dividing the said Province into parishes." The colonial assembly of the time had three factions: one that favored establishing the English Church; one that opposed such a measure in any form; and another faction that favored "no churches at all." But the opponents of Establishment were divided on other political issues as well, and Governor Ellis skillfully exploited those divisions to get the religious Establishment bill approved. The bill divided Georgia into eight ecclesiastical parishes (later to become twelve) that functioned also (and mainly) as civil administration units. Indeed, the parish vestries, along with the magistrates (Justices of the Peace) constituted the only form of local government in colonial Georgia. The English Church was thus established but not imposed, which is to say that all free male taxpayers in each parish—Dissenters as well as Anglicans—were granted the right to vote in vestry elections. This was indispensable to passage of the bill because the parish vestries had the authority to levy taxes for the relief of the poor and for maintaining Anglican Church buildings.

The Darien Scots' Old Meeting House

Some religious communities during the first quarter-century of the Georgia colony's existence had nothing worthy of being called a church or a synagogue. They either rented space or used public buildings for their services, or they met, probably, in private homes or in open air beneath trees. To be sure, the Scottish Presbyterians of the New Inverness (Darien) district had built for themselves a "Meeting House" near present-day Darien sometime before 1750, but "the Old Meeting House" could not be compared architecturally to, for example, Christ Church Savannah, which, as noted already, was consecrated in 1750. Nevertheless, the Scots' Old Meeting House was an important building in colonial and Revolutionary Georgia. It served not only as a church building but also as a gathering place for the colonists of Saint Andrew's Parish on public occasions. Indeed, it was in the Old Meeting House that the Darien Committee met in 1775 to select delegates to the Provincial Congress at Savannah and to adopt several resolutions favoring independence from Britain—that action pre-dating the passage of the famous Halifax Resolves in North Carolina in April 1776.

"Through many dangers, toils, and snares": The Baptists organize Kiokee Church

In the early 1770s, there lived a man by the name of Daniel Marshall in the Horse Creek Valley of west-central South Carolina, near Augusta. Mr. Marshall had been born in Windsor, Connecticut, in 1706, and brought up as a Congregationalist. During the Great Awakening (see p. 6), he became a Separate Baptist and was baptized in Winchester, Virginia. He later traveled to North Carolina to hear a well-known preacher of the day, and ended up settling there and marrying the preacher's sister. His ordination as a Baptist minister took place in North Carolina in 1757, and by 1770 he was living in South Carolina, whence he would, on occasion, push across the Savannah River into Georgia to preach to as-yet-unorganized Baptists. Then, for reasons that remain unclear, Mr. Marshall became the center of a drama in 1772.

While meeting with a group of Baptists one Sunday morning in a grove of trees in what is now Columbia County, he was kneeling in prayer in preparation for the morning services. Suddenly his devotions were interrupted when a hand fell heavily onto his shoulder, and a firm voice exclaimed, "You are my prisoner for preaching in the Parish of Saint Paul!" The arresting officer was Constable Samuel Cartlege. At Mr. Marshall's hearing before a magistrate in Augusta, he was ordered banished from the Royal Province of Georgia, not to return in the capacity of Baptist preacher. But he boldly replied, "Whether it be right to obey God or man, judge ye!" And, disregarding the court's order, he continued to preach in Georgia. His arrest was not strictly lawful, as he had broken no law, and the whole incident was likely the result of the personal enmity of some detractor of his. In any event, he was not molested by the authorities again, which may have had something to do with his wife's eloquent and passionate speech at the hearing before the magistrate in Augusta.

Mrs. Marshall seems to have been a forceful personality, literate and educated. At the hearing, she had made quite a stirring speech—a ringing denunciation of the very idea of an Established Church—and she had spoken with power in defense of freedom of conscience, repeatedly quoting the Scriptures in support of her arguments. The arresting officer, Constable Cartlege, later revealed that he had been deeply affected by Mrs. Marshall's speech before the court that day. Five years later, Cartlege himself abandoned the English Church and became a member of Kiokee Baptist Church, which had been organized under Mr. Marshall's leadership in 1772, making it Georgia's first and oldest Baptist church.

But that's not all. Eventually Constable Cartlege became the Rev. Mr. Cartlege, one of early Georgia's most important and influential Baptist clergymen. And to top it all off, he was ordained by Daniel Marshall, whom he himself had arrested only a few years earlier for being a Baptist preacher!

Kiokee Church was incorporated by act of the Georgia legislature in 1789. Their small, very refined, slate-roofed brick building, completed in 1808, still stands in the woods of Columbia County, a few miles from Appling, the county seat. It belongs to the congregation and is well maintained by them but is no longer in regular use because they have a larger and more modern building in Appling.

The Revolution disestablishes the Church of England

The American Revolution broke out in 1775, with the fighting at Lexington and Concord, Massachusetts ("the shot heard round the world"). The Declaration of Independence came in 1776, and Georgia accordingly formed a Revolutionary government in 1777. The 1777 Constitution of Georgia disestablished the Church of England, guaranteed official toleration for the religions of all (including Roman Catholics), and converted the twelve ecclesiastical parishes of the colonial period into the eight original counties of the newly independent state of Georgia. The Revolution officially ended with the signing of the Treaty of Paris in 1783.

Georgia's churches were prostrate. Even the formerly vigorous Lutheran congregations in Effingham County were without pastors, and the Anglican clergy, too, had left Georgia. Some congregations of other denominations managed somehow to hang together despite the lack of clergy and the turbulent conditions that naturally follow any revolution, but for all practical purposes, organized religion had ceased to exist in Georgia by the end of the Revolution. Only the Quakers at Wrightsborough and the Baptists continued to function at all normally.

After the Revolution

The Baptists of Georgia had become numerous enough to effect administrative separation from South Carolina Baptists as early as 1785, but they were the only religious community in Georgia that was strong enough to do so at such an early date.

In 1785, the Georgia General Assembly passed a law that was an attempt at a compromise between an established church and religious liberty. The law provided for the election of clergymen by the voters of each county and for the elected county clergy then to be paid by the state. The law stipulated equal liberty and toleration for all denominations, but it never went into effect.

"Marching to Zion": The Methodists organize Liberty Church

The Methodist Church formed in Baltimore in 1784. About the same time, Georgia Methodists organized their first congregation, Liberty Church in Richmond County. The present-day Liberty Church building dates from 1804 and remains in regular use.

Georgia's Methodists enjoyed such phenomenal membership growth in the 1780s and 1790s that, although the first Methodist ministers arrived in Georgia as late as 1785, by 1788 Bishop Francis Asbury was presiding over Georgia's first Methodist Conference, which was held in Wilkes County. In 1790, the Methodists introduced the then-new practice of "campground" into Georgia, with the establishment in Effingham County of a permanent site for camp meetings. Camp meetings are still held there to this day, every August.

Slavery and the churches

As a rule, slaves belonged to their owners' congregations. In Savannah and Augusta, however, before the close of the eighteenth century, black congregations were permitted to form and to govern themselves independently, but these were exceptions to the rule. Such an idea was tried by Bethesda Baptist Church in Greene County, for example, early in the nineteenth century, but the practice was stopped almost as soon as it began (See www.bethesda1.homestead.com/history.html). Independent black congregations would come along only after the abolition of slavery. A noteworthy and well-known exception is, of course, Springfield Baptist Church, still worshiping in downtown Augusta and now well into its third century of independence. It was at Springfield Church in Augusta that Atlanta's Morehouse College was born in 1867 as the Augusta Institute. It moved to Atlanta in 1879.

"Faith of our fathers": Georgia's first Catholic congregation is organized

After Georgia ratified the Constitution of the United States in 1788 and began making liberal land grants to attract new settlers, more and more Catholics felt willing to settle in Georgia. In 1790, a group of Marylanders of English extraction settled in a part of Wilkes County that is now Taliaferro County and established Georgia's first Roman Catholic Congregation: the Church of the Purification (see www.hrcga.org/).

Their settlement was called Locust Grove, and their first priest was Father John Lemoin, who came to Georgia from Baltimore. The Locust Grove community was augmented in 1800 by the arrival of French refugees, fleeing the revolution in France and slave insurrections in Santo Domingo (Haiti). Many of the French refugees were members of the nobility, and they brought with them another priest, a Father Sujet. The French refugees included the families of Menard, Belliance, Rossignol du Perry, Printière, de Loucy, and others. Very shortly after the arrival of the French, a group of Irish Catholics also arrived in Locust Grove to join the Catholic settlement there. Eventually, most of the French families moved to other parts of Georgia.

Georgia's first Catholic school, Locust Grove Academy, was established about 1818. Many distinguished Georgians were educated there, including Alexander Hamilton Stephens, who would eventually become Vice President of the Confederate States of America.

In 1821, Father John England was appointed pastor of the Church of the Purification. Dr. England was such an inspiring preacher that people of all faiths came from miles around to hear him.

Eventually, the Irish members of the community were decimated by Yellow Fever, and finally, in 1877, under the direction of a Father O'Brien, the Church of the Purification moved from Locust Grove into Sharon to be nearer to the people, since the Protestant population of Taliaferro County had greatly increased.

The congregation continues to function today at Sharon (Taliaferro County) and is therefore the oldest Roman Catholic congregation in Georgia.

It ought to be recalled that outside of Maryland and a few isolated spots, there was no appreciable Roman Catholic presence in British America. Indeed, there was no Roman Catholic house of worship in

America before 1720. The strong Roman Catholic presence in America today is largely the result of the 19th- and 20th-century immigration from Ireland and from eastern and southern Europe. Therefore it is noteworthy that today the largest church building in rural Georgia is a Roman Catholic church: the abbey church of the Monastery of the Holy Spirit in Rockdale County.

The Nineteenth Century

Georgia was still by and large a frontier state in 1820, by which date the Baptists were still the only denomination independent of ecclesiastical authorities in South Carolina. Others would have to wait until their numbers grew sufficiently large to allow them to run their own affairs from within the boundaries of Georgia. And there were still many persons in Georgia in the 1820s who were not members of any church, whether from indifference or from lack of opportunity remains unclear. Georgians at the time were interested in clearing the land, getting rid of the Indians, and increasing their wealth. Building fine churches could wait.

As the nineteenth century progressed, the Presbyterians, Episcopalians, Lutherans, and the Disciples of Christ began to grow in numbers and strength, although never matching the vigor of the Methodists and Baptists in that arena. The Irish of colonial Georgia had been almost wholly Protestant, but by 1850, so many Irish Catholics had immigrated into Georgia that the Catholic Diocese of Savannah was formed. By 1860, about 6500 Irish Catholics lived in Georgia, most of them in Savannah, where one third of the free population was foreign-born. The Jewish community in Savannah continued to grow slowly as a few immigrants arrived from Germany. The Christians and Jews of Georgia became increasingly partisan along with the rest of the population in the years leading up to secession and war in the 1860s. More than a few of the clergy and the people opposed secession, but once Georgia had left the Union and cast her lot with the Confederacy, Georgians of all religions stoutly supported the Cause of Southern Independence.

The collapse of the Confederacy left Georgia's churches in disarray. Many church buildings had been destroyed or damaged, and others were dilapidated simply because of the economic dislocation caused by war. Many churches had been used as hospitals by both sides, and Federal troops had vandalized and desecrated many of Georgia's churches, just as the British had done during the Revolution. After the war, Federal authorities closed down some churches when the clergy and people refused to pray for the President of the United States. Blacks withdrew themselves from white churches after the war and began to form their own congregations, and religion, which, before the war, had been completely integrated racially, became completely segregated afterwards. But the South's defeat in war had given to religion a significance that it had not formerly had in Georgia, and congregations, both black and white, proliferated, with Baptists and Methodists reaping the greatest harvests. Revival meetings, singing conventions (notably Shape-Note, or "Sacred Harp" singing), and weekly church services assumed importance as social events as well as religious ones. Most of rural Georgia's interesting examples of church architecture date from the 19th century.

Twentieth & twenty-first centuries

As the nineteenth century gave way to the twentieth, urbanization and the emigration of whites and blacks began to take their toll on rural Georgia. By the 1950s, churches had ceased in general to play the dominant role in the social life of rural Georgians, and churches declined in membership and in many cases were abandoned. World wars introduced many Georgians, both urban and rural, to things theretofore undreamt of by them, and paved roads and the flowering of the automobile culture made city attractions a powerful draw for many. The old rural South was passing, giving way to an urban age.

Nevertheless, religion has managed to maintain a central role in the life of a great many Georgians, if not most. In fact, religious affiliation has reached its high point in the post-World-War-II period, with nearly 45% of the population claiming membership in some organized religious community. Baptists and Methodists continue to dominate among both whites and blacks, with Baptists accounting for about one Georgian out of four. Increasing urbanization may have caused the social role of the churches to decline, but with approximately 7000 white Protestant churches, 3000 black Protestant churches, and scores of Roman Catholic and Jewish congregations, a great many Georgians have kept participation in organized religion at the center of their lives. The challenge is for those who support the preservation of historic buildings to maintain rural Georgia's heritage of ecclesiastical architecture. But with the advent of personal computers and the concomitant possibility of "telecommuting" (working at home), it is not too much to hope that rural Georgia may one day soon experience a renaissance. It is hoped, too, that should a renaissance occur, it will bring with it the preservation of the many culturally invaluable examples of both domestic and ecclesiastical architecture in the rural parts of our state.

Architectural heritage endangered

Even so, it was precisely the prosperity of the 1980s and 1990s that caused a great deal of damage to culturally important buildings in rural areas as congregations had the money to indulge their quite natural desire to modernize their property. Air conditioning and central heating are, of course, improvements in anybody's book, and even vinyl siding has been installed on some buildings in sensitive and appropriate ways. But prosperity also allowed some congregations to introduce stained glass into some buildings that are not suitable for stained glass—especially the inferior stained glass that one so often encounters. And the Americans With Disabilities Act has been the cause of unfortunate alterations in a great many historic churches as rural congregations are obliged to attach sometimes-unsightly ramps to formerly unspoiled 18th- and 19th-century structures.

It is the purpose of this book to encourage an interest in and a familiarity with rural Georgia's heritage of church architecture, with a view towards giving an impetus, however slight, to the preservation of these important—and irreplaceable—buildings. The landscape of rural Georgia would be inconceivable without them. This book is not intended as an exhaustive or scholarly study, but rather merely as a survey and overview of the subject. My survey was limited—quite arbitrarily—to bona fide rural areas or to towns with populations of about 20,000 inhabitants or fewer. This book is written with the hope that the field will be studied in the future by someone better qualified than I to undertake the effort with credibility. A video documentary would be of enormous cultural and historical value.

Religious reforms produce changes in architecture

The Protestant Reformation of the Church brought forward theological ideas that demanded changes in public worship and therefore in ecclesiastical architecture. The Lutheran and Anglican reformers retained the traditional, ancient liturgical and architectural forms until Rationalism and Pietism began to take their toll, but, having survived those movements, would eventually restore them. But the Reformed churches did not retain the traditional forms, and it was, after all, Reformed theology that would come to dominate religious life in the United States, especially after the Great Awakening and the Revolution. This was to have important implications for American church architecture.

Cultural and theological influences on building styles

By the end of the first quarter of the eighteenth century, when the Georgia colony was established, the Age of Enlightenment and the Industrial Revolution were already underway, and political revolutions in America and France were not far off. The religious struggles and wars of sixteenth- and seventeenth-century Europe, combined with the far-reaching effects of the Enlightenment, the Industrial Revolution, and of philosophical and theological Rationalism, would bring religious life on both sides of the Atlantic to a low ebb in the eighteenth and nineteenth centuries. For Protestants of every stripe and in every country,

Holy Communion would come to be rather a rare event, and listening to sermons would take its place as the chief act of Christian worship on Sundays (a fact with which John Wesley, during his tempestuous sojourn in Georgia, would have to contend). Moral improvement came to be seen as more important than inner experience. Reading newspapers replaced the recitation of the ancient morning prayers. The various Puritan movements would give birth to Deism and Unitarianism as the work of Sir Isaac Newton (and others) and the material successes of Science began to penetrate the popular consciousness.

In New England, the Puritans even made it unlawful to celebrate Christmas just as puritanical elements in American society in our own day have tried to do by banning manger scenes and other religious displays on public property such as court house lawns. The religious ideas and sentiments current during the late seventeenth and early eighteenth centuries found voice in the sermons of Cotton and Increase Mather, Jonathan Edwards, and George Whitefield. Voltaire would advise the adoption of a simple, "natural" religion in place of traditional Christianity. These developments alone would have assured that religious practices and architecture would change, even apart from the effects of the trans-Atlantic transplantation of an entire culture.

Frontier conditions, of course, made impossible from the beginning the intact transplantation of the traditional European and British styles and forms of ecclesiastical architecture. Nevertheless, in Europe as well as in America, the pulpit began to replace the altar as the most prominent furnishing in the church, and the chancel disappeared from many new buildings. Two of the traditionally liturgical Protestant churches pictured in this book were built during the time that these theological and liturgical ideas and practices held sway, and they retain today their original arrangements, in which the pulpit has an equally central location with the altar (see Jerusalem Lutheran and Grace-Calvary Episcopal churches). Such examples of eighteenth- and early nineteenth-century ecclesiastical architecture may be seen here and there throughout the Atlantic Coast states and in England even today.

Influence of the Oxford Movement

In 1833, John Keble preached his famous sermon *The National Apostasy* in Oxford, England, thus beginning the Oxford Movement, which, along with the work of the Wesleys and others, would revitalize ecclesiastical life in England for a time. At that same time, there was a revival of interest in and use of the Gothic style of architecture, not only for churches, but also for homes and for such public buildings as the old Georgia Capitol in Milledgeville. The thrust of the Oxford Movement was to restore to the Church of England some of the doctrines and practices that had been neglected since the Reformation, and Gothic Revival architecture, with its medieval feeling and inspiration, dovetailed naturally and perfectly with the ideas of the "Tractarians" who constituted the Oxford Movement. The Oxford Movement and the revival of the Gothic style were rich sources for architects and builders of churches throughout the nineteenth century. It was felt somehow that there was a connection between Christian spirituality and the Gothic style—that the Gothic style was somehow more appropriate for church architecture than the neoclassical style of the seventeenth and eighteenth centuries because the Gothic had developed during the Middle Ages and in "Christian Europe" and in the service of the Church. Churches built in this style were intentionally dark and mysterious in atmosphere. But it would take decades for the influences of the Oxford Movement and the Gothic Revival style in architecture to manifest themselves in the church buildings of Georgia. When those influences did make themselves felt, they produced such buildings as Zion Episcopal Church in Talbotton (c. 1848); Mediator Episcopal Church in Washington-Wilkes (c. 1896); and St. Michael's Episcopal Church in Waynesboro (c. 1894). (See below, "More examples.")

A vernacular style develops

The general cultural and religious climate engendered by the Protestant Reformation of the sixteenth and seventeenth centuries, by the Great Awakening of the eighteenth century, and by frontier conditions would produce a completely new style of ecclesiastical architecture in America and, more to the point, in Georgia. This "vernacular style" became ubiquitous: a simple, even severe, one-room, rectangular wooden frame meeting house with end gables and with two main doors, one for men and one for women. Porches, towers, and spires were usually absent, especially when a building was first built. (A one-room church is one whose floor is all one one level, although perhaps with a dais at one end. A two-room church usually has one or two floor levels at one end that are raised above the main part of the floor and enclosed by a railing within which stands an altar or communion table.) Such features as towers and spires were added later in many cases. There are hundreds of such buildings throughout Georgia today, but perhaps the oldest and best example of the plain vernacular style in wood is Liberty Methodist Church (c. 1804) in Richmond County. There are many variations on the basic plain-style theme throughout the state. For example, the Washington Presbyterian Church building (Wilkes County) began its existence in 1825 with an appearance very much like that of Liberty Methodist Church in Richmond County, but as increasingly settled conditions and increasing prosperity allowed for later additions of a tower, a spire, and a porch, the building eventually gained its present degree of elegant sophistication. Greene County's Bethesda Baptist Church (c. 1818) is virtually identical to Liberty Methodist and to Washington Presbyterian in its basic design, but it is of somewhat larger proportions and is built of brick rather than of the far more frequently employed wood, and it reaches an unusually high degree of substantiality and refinement. Also, like the Congregational church in Midway, Bethesda Church has two tiers of windows to accommodate the slave galleries that formerly wrapped around three of the interior walls. Another perfect example of the plain style in brick is Kiokee Baptist Church (c. 1808) in Columbia County.

Jerusalem Lutheran Church (c. 1769) in Effingham County is a yet more elaborate variation on the basic vernacular-style church building. It possesses the one-room rectangular meeting house form with end gables just as do Liberty Methodist, Washington Presbyterian, Bethesda Baptist, Kiokee Baptist, and scores or even hundreds of others. Like Bethesda and Kiokee, it is of brick, and it has a belfry reminiscent of the one on Midway Congregational Church (c. 1792; Liberty County). The impressive proportions, clean lines, and refinement of detail make Jerusalem Lutheran Church one of Georgia's finest buildings, old or new.

Other excellent examples in wood include Ways Baptist (c. 1840; Jefferson County); Clarkesville Presbyterian (c. 1838; Habersham County); Grace-Calvary Episcopal (c. 1838; Habersham County); Old Emory Methodist in Oxford (c. 1841; Newton County); the Presbyterian and Methodist churches in Saint Mary's (Camden County; c. 1808 & 1860); and many others throughout the state.

The persistence of the vernacular style is illustrated by the many twentieth-century examples, both in wood and in brick, throughout the state. However, changes in religious ideas, customs, and practices, and changes in technology are combining nowadays to produce a new form of architecture for religious use in Georgia and, of course, elsewhere. The term "worship space" is used increasingly to describe what only a decade or two ago would have been called a church. The introduction of "rock" music into Christian worship over the last 45 years, with its reliance on electronically amplified sound, has produced "worship spaces" that double as gymnasiums or that merely look like gymnasiums or even, in many cases, like theatres, with a stage at one end. As the Church continues to conform herself to popular culture, worship becomes louder and ever more theatrical, demanding changes in architecture. Examples abound, particularly in urban areas. One excellent rural example (semi-rural, anyway) is the Harvest Temple Church of God near Griffin (Spalding County). This imposing masonry structure was completed about 1988, and it is well worth a visit by those interested in trends in modern church architecture.

More examples

Cruciform two-room churches in rural Georgia that also were influenced by the Oxford Movement in theology and by the Gothic Revival style in architecture are Saint Michael's Episcopal Church in Waynesboro (Burke County); and Christ Episcopal Church on Saint Simon's Island (Glynn County). Both are in the Queen Anne style, popular during the late Victorian era. Brick buildings with stained glass such as Bethabara Baptist Church (c. 1910; Oconee County); the First Baptist Church of McRae (c. 1908; Telfair County); and the Presbyterian Church in Quitman (c. 1909; Brooks County) belong to the twentieth century. The Presbyterian Church in Quitman and the Temple Bethel synagogue in Bainbridge (c. 1916; Decatur County) are fine examples of the influence of the Beaux Arts style, which reached the apex of its development just before the Great War of 1914–1918.

Soli Deo Gloria

A Survey of Church Architecture in Rural Georgia

The Illustrations

1. Jerusalem Lutheran Church (c. 1769), Effingham County
2. Episcopal Church of the Advent (c. 1842), Madison, Morgan County
3. Piney Grove Missionary Baptist Church (date unk.), Thomas County
4. Old Mercer University Chapel (c. 1841), Penfield, Greene County
5. Washington Presbyterian Church (c. 1825), Washington, Wilkes County
6. Episcopal Church of the Redeemer (c. 1868), Greensboro, Greene County
7. All Saints Episcopal Church (date uncertain), Thomasville, Thomas County
8. Old Stone Church (c. 1850), Catoosa County
9. Abbey Church (c. 1945), Monastery of the Holy Spirit, Rockdale County
10. Hebron Presbyterian Church (early 20th cent.), Franklin County
11. Madison Presbyterian Church (c. 1842), Madison, Morgan County
12. Saint Mary's Presbyterian Church (c. 1808), Saint Mary's, Camden County
13. Saint Cyprian's Episcopal Church (c. 1875), Darien, McIntosh County
14. Bethesda Baptist Church (c. 1818), Greene County
15. Zion Episcopal Church (c. 1848), Talbotton, Talbot County
16. Damascus Methodist Church (c. 1878), Westville, Stewart County
17. Kiokee Baptist Church (c. 1808), Columbia County
18. Episcopal Church of the Mediator (c. 1896), Washington, Wilkes County
19. Midway Congregational Church (c. 1792), Midway, Liberty County
20. Liberty Methodist Church (c. 1804), Hephzibah, Richmond County
21. Old Emory University Chapel (c. 1841), Oxford, Newton County
22. Temple Bethel (c. 1920) Bainbridge, Decatur County
23. Grace-Calvary Episcopal Church (c. 1842), Clarkesville, Habersham County

24. Catholic Church of the Purification (c. 1883), Sharon (Taliaferro County)
25. Bethabara Baptist Church (c. 1910), Oconee County

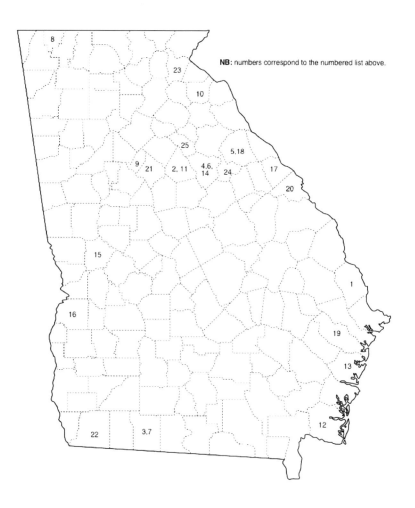

A Survey of Church Architecture in Rural Georgia

Jerusalem Lutheran Church (Effingham County) is the oldest public building in Georgia. Built by the Salzburgers' own hands (see Introduction), the building has remained in continuous use since its completion in 1769. The bells in the tower, brought from Europe, are the oldest in Georgia, and they remain in regular use. The masonry structure is 80 feet long and 60 feet wide. Its 21-inch-thick walls are built of handmade bricks that are laid in English bond. Some of the original glass remains in the 20-over-20 windows despite the depredations of British troops during the Revolution and of Federal troops during the War Between the States. Note the delicately flared line of the roof at the eaves and the wrap-around band of iron about halfway up the wall. The Salzburgers produced lumber for the construction at their own sawmill, and they made the bricks from nearby deposits of red clay. On the front exterior wall of the building, slightly to the left of the main entrance door, one may see the finger-marks of little children's hands in a brick from where they handled the brick before it was fully dried. The Salzburgers established Georgia's first Sunday school here (1734) and built Georgia's first orphanage (1737). The Georgia Salzburger Society maintains a museum on the church grounds, where visitors may see the original communion chalice that the settlers brought with them in 1734 from Europe. Also on view is the last surviving colonial-era Salzburger home. Today, descendants of the original Salzburger colonists continue to populate the vicinity and to worship regularly in this most historic building. The building is surely one of the most significant in the United States.

How Firm a Foundation

Another view of the exterior, Jerusalem Lutheran Church, 1769 (Effingham County).

Interior detail, Jerusalem Lutheran Church, showing the typical 18th-century central placement of both altar and pulpit (cf. Grace-Calvary Episcopal Church, Clarkesville). Also, although a Lutheran Church, there is no chancel floor (cf. Zion Episcopal Church, Talbotton).

A Survey of Church Architecture in Rural Georgia

The Episcopal Church of the Advent, Madison (Morgan County), was built as the town's Methodist church (c. 1842). The solid masonry structure is a vernacular expression of the Gothic Revival style. The tower and spire project forward, thus emphasizing the single entrance door that is itself emphasized by means of the pointed arch that encloses it.

(Above and Right) Episcopal Church of the Advent, Madison (Morgan County), c. 1842. Extensive renovations were undertaken beginning in 1961. The altar railing and balcony were kept intact, but the reredos, apse, and ambulatory were added at that time, as was the rear entry (not visible). The graceful wrought-iron chandeliers are older than the building. New pews, altar, and other appointments were purchased at the time of the renovations. The renovations managed to harmonize the neoclassical revival details of the interior with the Gothic Revival details of the building itself (especially the lancet windows) to produce a very pleasing whole.

A Survey of Church Architecture in Rural Georgia

A visit to Piney Grove Missionary Baptist Church (Thomas County) is a delight. The beautifully aged copper sheathing on the spire, the refined details of the ribbed entrance doors, the elegant finials on the tower, and the graceful window under the porch combine to produce a building with a good deal of sophistication that is surprising because it stands quite literally in the middle of the woods. But even more pleasing than the elegance and sophistication of the details of construction is the perfect proportionality of the parts to one another and to the whole. Even the surrounding trees themselves are in perfect proportion to the building, so that the building seems to have sprouted and grown there among them. Even the size of the clearing and the length and width of the approach are in perfect proportion to the building. To see how harmonious the proportion and lines truly are, try this: Look at the photo, and try to imagine the structure, first, without the belfry and spire, but still with the square tower where it rises above the roof. Then, try to imagine the building with neither spire nor belfry nor the portion of the tower above the roof. It is plain to see that whether with tower and spire, or with the tower only, or without either feature, the main part of the structure would be just as beautiful and just as elegant because the roof-top embellishments harmonize with one another and with the main part of the structure as well, and also because the proportions and lines of the main part of the structure are so perfect in and by themselves. As good and faithful stewards, the members of this historically black congregation maintain the building beautifully. A real gem.

How Firm a Foundation

The light, elegant lines of the window under the porch provide the perfect balance to the imposing ribbed entrance doors that flank the window on both sides. The window's rounded, or fan-shaped, arch and its placement in a projection, or pavilion (actually the base of the tower), give the whole a Palladian flavor. Very pleasing.

A Survey of Church Architecture in Rural Georgia

The copper-sheathed spire caps a very finely detailed open belfry that houses a diminutive bell. The belfry rises from a square tower that is capped by a balustrade with simple, square balusters, and by a finial at each corner of the tower. Superb.

How Firm a Foundation

The old chapel of Mercer University, occupying the high point of a hill overlooking the highway through Penfield (Greene County), still dominates the quadrangle where Mercer University's original academic and residential buildings used to stand. Established here at Penfield in 1833, Mercer University did not move to Macon until 1871. This massive masonry building (c. 1841) is an impressive vernacular expression of the Greek Revival style. The church's massive Doric columns are of plaster over brick.

(RIGHT) The square Doric pilasters under the porch roof are echoed in wood at the four corners of the sturdy spire that sits atop the roof. The front gable is continued, to form an enclosed pediment whose lack of architectural adornment emphasizes the post-and-lintel construction methods of the ancient Greeks. The generously proportioned windows have 48 panes over 48, with louvered shutters to darken and cool the interior. Most of the glass is original. The building is one of Georgia's most important architectural and cultural treasures. The home of Jesse Mercer still stands behind the building, which is now home to the Penfield Baptist Church. Also on the site is the present-day Penfield Home, which is operated by the Georgia Baptist Convention. The nearby Penfield Baptist Cemetery is so beautifully laid out and maintained that there is likely no lovelier churchyard anywhere in Georgia, with the possible exceptions of Ways Baptist (Jefferson County) and Midway Congregational (Liberty County). In the Penfield cemetery, Jesse Mercer and other prominent early Georgia Baptists are buried. Both church and cemetery are well worth a visit.

A Survey of Church Architecture in Rural Georgia

How Firm a Foundation

The Washington Presbyterian Church, Washington (Wilkes County), was built in 1825. Originally similar in appearance to most other vernacular-style rural church buildings (see Introduction), it has been embellished with the present-day classical details by succeeding generations. One former minister of the congregation is buried underneath the floor of the narthex (the marble monument visible at the extreme left of the narthex photo).

A Survey of Church Architecture in Rural Georgia

The wooden cross above the pulpit was made from the wood of the "Presbyterian Poplar," as were the offering collection plates. The Presbyterian Poplar stood about one mile from the church, and it was under its branches that Georgia's first Presbyterian ordination ceremony took place (1790), when the Rev. Mr. Springer was ordained to serve the Washington congregation and two other congregations in Wilkes County. When the tree finally died in the 1940s, the wood was used to make the cross and the collection plates.

The church's small pipe organ is a rare and wonderful instrument.

How Firm a Foundation

Organized in 1863, the congregation of Redeemer Episcopal Church, Greensboro (Greene County), first met in members' homes. In 1867, the church-wardens bought a lot for $100 on which to build a church. Construction was completed in 1868 under the direction of architect and builder J. G. Barnwell of Rome, Georgia. The church building has a couple of unusual features, including the roof line, which flares delicately at the eaves (cf. Jerusalem Lutheran Church, Effingham County), and the hand-blown glass in the intricate diamond-pane windows. The unusual red color was the original from 1868, a fact that was discovered during restoration work in 1989 and 1990.

(TOP RIGHT) Formerly St. Augustine's Roman Catholic Church, this building was moved by truck to its present location and was completely refurbished for use by the congregation of All Saints Episcopal Church in Thomasville (Thomas County). The building has the typical end gable, but its cornice continues across the façade to form an enclosed pediment that is decorated with dentil blocks. The Victorian-style porch, the small spire atop the roof, and the subdued color scheme all combine to produce rather a sophisticated expression of the typical vernacular style.

A Survey of Church Architecture in Rural Georgia

(BELOW) The Old Stone Church near Ringgold (Catoosa County) was built in 1850 of sandstone quarried nearby. The Presbyterian congregation was organized in 1837, even before the Cherokee were removed from the area. The congregation, the first in the county, was made up of Scotch-Irish settlers from the Carolinas and Tennessee. During the Battle of Ringgold (1864), the church was used as a hospital. It remained a Presbyterian church until about 1920, when it was bought by a Methodist congregation. Descendants of the original church members bought the building after the Second World War and deeded it to a board of trustees to be used for religious purposes. It has been used most recently by a Baptist congregation.

How Firm a Foundation

The abbey church of the Monastery of the Holy Spirit (Rockdale County) was built circa 1945 by the brothers of the Trappist Order who had moved to Georgia from Kentucky to establish a community in rural Georgia. It is the largest church building in rural Georgia, built by the brothers' own hands in a pleasing style that blends Gothic with modern elements. Located near Interstate 20 on the eastern edge of metropolitan Atlanta, the monastery attracts a great many visitors every year. Note the cloister (extending to the right), where the brothers live, attached to the nave (left) of the church.

The nave of the abbey church, Monastery of the Holy Spirit, Rockdale County (c. 1945). The etymology and meaning of the word "nave" is here made delightfully apparent. The medieval concept of the Church as "the ship of salvation" is intimately bound up with the architectural design and building methods that produce the style we call "Gothic." You can see quite clearly here the inverted hull of a great sailing-ship (turn the picture upside-down). Hence the word "nave" (<L. *navis*, "ship") for the middle part, or body, of a church building, where the worshipers sit or stand. An outstanding example.

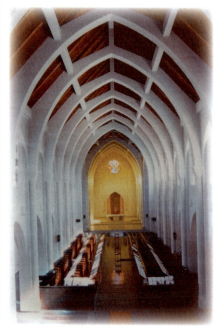

Monastery of the Holy Spirit (c. 1945), Rockdale County.

This view is of the main, or western, front with its great portal. Visible on the left in the background is a portion of the North Transcept. In the foreground may be seen a portion of the cloister, which is attached to the church.

Hebron Presbyterian Church (Franklin County) was established in 1796. The present building, an excellent example of the typical, simple one-room meeting house with end gables, dates from the early 20th century. Here, the building is seen from the church yard, which is dominated by a number of mysterious and fascinating cairns.

A Survey of Church Architecture in Rural Georgia

The Madison Presbyterian Church, in Madison (Morgan County), is a Greek Revival-style building of simple, classical dignity. It was built in 1842 for the Presbyterians of Madison by a remarkably skilled mason, one Daniel Killian, according to church records. Note the open front gable cornice and the Doric pilasters that frame the doorways and support a continuous entablature that is decorated with dentil blocks. Note, too, the repetition of those same details on the square tower. The original nine-over-nine windows remain in the front of the building, but the main windows along the sides of the church were replaced in 1875 with stained glass windows that were themselves replaced in 1908 with the elaborate Tiffany stained glass that we see today. The silver communion service was stolen by Federal troops during the invasion of Georgia in 1864, but it was returned many, many years later by kind Northerners, and it remains today in the congregation's loving possession.

A Survey of Church Architecture in Rural Georgia

Detail: Tiffany stained-glass. Madison Presbyterian Church, Madison (Morgan County).

A Survey of Church Architecture in Rural Georgia

Detail. Madison Presbyterian Church (Morgan County). Tiffany stained-glass, showing lead and glass construction method.

The Presbyterian Church in Saint Mary's (Camden County) was built in 1808 at a cost of about $3500 on land donated by the city of Saint Mary's. Originally, the building was used by all citizens of the town, becoming exclusively Presbyterian in 1828. Damaged by fire in 1956, the church was restored with advice from Dr. Thomas Little, a consultant on the Georgia Historical Commission. Dr. Little described the building as "the finest example of early church architecture...in Georgia and one of the finest...in the United States. It is truly a work of art..., executed by...craftsmen. [It was] created to last for centuries."

A Survey of Church Architecture in Rural Georgia

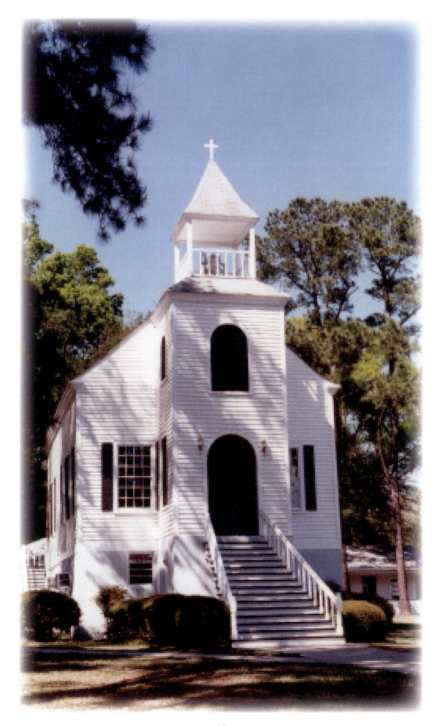

Saint Cyprian's Episcopal Church (c. 1876), Darien (McIntosh County), is a cruciform two-room church (see Introduction) built of tabby, brick, and wood. It is one of the finest and most interesting of all historically black churches in Georgia, rural or urban. It was built "for the colored people of McIntosh County" under the leadership of James Wentworth Leigh, DD, FSA, who was the Dean of Hereford Cathedral in England. Contributions for construction were received from England and from Philadelphia as well as from local citizens. It was consecrated in April 1876 and stands in the historic town of Darien, overlooking the mighty Altamaha River. Note the tabby buttresses that divide the exterior wall of the nave into three bays between the tower and the transcepts and the clever use of brick to finish and set off the windows. The congregation is named in honor of Cyprian, a third-century bishop of Carthage who also was an early martyr for the Christian faith on the continent of Africa.

A Survey of Church Architecture in Rural Georgia

How Firm a Foundation

Saint Cyprian's Church, Darien (McIntosh County). Below, note tabby construction.

A Survey of Church Architecture in Rural Georgia

Bethesda Baptist Church, in Greene County, near Union Point, is without doubt one of Georgia's architectural treasures — one of the finest, oldest, and most imposing country churches in the entire Deep South. Completed in 1818 for a congregation established in 1785, the elegant building is of bricks that were molded and fired on site, the plentiful red clay of Georgia providing the raw material. The impressions of human fingers, which may be seen in some of the bricks, were made when slaves carried incompletely dried bricks from mold to firing oven. The two tiers of windows were necessary to accommodate the slave gallery that wrapped around three walls of the interior in former times (see also Midway Congregational Church, Liberty County). The front gable cornice of this vernacular-style building is left open, typical of most vernacular-style churches in rural Georgia. The major differences here are the use of brick instead of wood and the double tier of windows. The four original, massive fireplaces have been retained in the interior as have the huge iron brackets by the entrance doors that were used to bar the doors against Indian attack in earlier times. The brick walls, laid in American, or common, bond, are twenty-four inches thick from the foundation up to the top of the lower tier of windows, and eighteen inches thick from there to the ceiling. Most of the windows contain the original hand-blown glass panes, and the shutters, too, are mostly original. The building was restored and refurbished lovingly and sensitively in preparation for the congregation's bi-centennial celebration in 1985. A real must-see.

How Firm a Foundation

Zion Episcopal Church, Talbotton (Talbot County), has been altered through the years less than perhaps any other church building in rural Georgia except for the Kiokee Baptist Church in Columbia County, q.v. The church has its roots in the missionary efforts of the Rev. Mr. Richard Johnson and the financial support of South Carolina rice planters. It is without doubt one of the most significant buildings in Georgia. The original Pilcher organ (1850), which operated on a bellows that still

has to be pumped by hand, still stands in its loft overlooking the main floor and still produces a pleasing sound. With its fifteen decorated and gilded pipes, it presents a charming appearance. The Gothic Revival structure, built between 1848 and 1853 by first-rate craftsmen under the direction of an unknown builder, is entirely of native Georgia heart pine and walnut. Even the altar cross is wooden. Interestingly, the star-shaped details that appear at the tops of the windows in Zion Church are remarkably similar to those that decorate the balustrade around the top of the campanile of the Duomo (cathedral) in Florence, Italy. Perhaps the builders of Zion Church had a pattern-book at their disposal. Indeed, according to historian Mills Lane (see Reading List), Zion Church may have been copied from an illustration in the influential *Ecclesiologist Magazine*, which was first published in 1841. The box pews, original to the structure, are rare in Georgia. This building is one of the few wooden church buildings of its era and style remaining in the United States. It was consecrated in 1853 by the Right Reverend Stephen Elliot, first Episcopal Bishop of Georgia.

Zion Episcopal Church (1848), Talbotton (Talbot County). Often, churches in the Gothic Revival style were painted gray or, as here, brown.

A Survey of Church Architecture in Rural Georgia

Zion Church. Nave and sanctuary. This building has no chancel (cf. Jerusalem Lutheran Church, Effingham County). Note the rare box pews (cf. Grace-Calvary Church, Clarkesville, Habersham County). The elaborate, exposed ceiling beams (not visible here) are remarkable.

Zion Episcopal Church, Talbotton. (Talbot County). 1848.

Zion Episcopal Church, Talbotton (detail). The narthex, showing the main entrance door and the stairs to the organ loft.

The 1850 Pilcher organ still produces a pleasing sound.

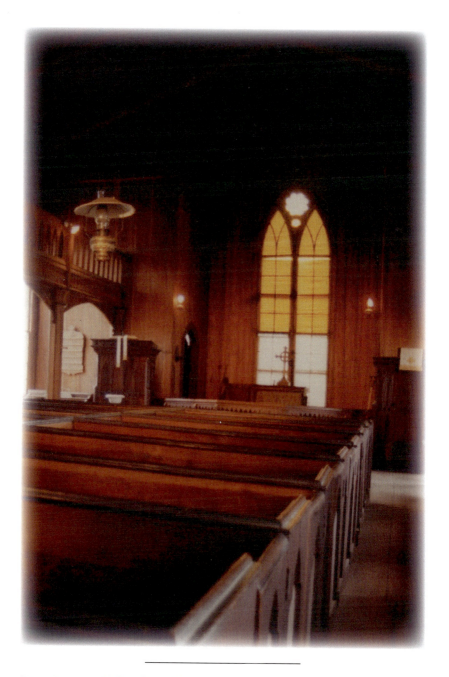

Zion Episcopal Church, Talbotton. (Talbot County). 1848. Looking up the nave. Note the fine craftsmanship of the box pews of native Georgia walnut.

A Survey of Church Architecture in Rural Georgia

Damascus Methodist Church (Stewart County) is a fine example of the typically plain one-room meeting-house-style churches seen throughout Georgia. The simple frame building (c. 1878) with four side bays was moved to its present location in Lumpkin (outside the gates of Westville) in 1983 from another part of Stewart County. The continuous front-gable cornice is unadorned. Indeed, the exterior appearance is almost severe in its lack of adornment—a fact that gives no hint of the amazing, painted folk-art decorations that enliven the interior.

An unknown itinerant painter accomplished the decorative interior painting that is the highlight of this building. Such painting was popular in the 19th century although rare in southwestern Georgia. Indeed, it is probably unique in Georgia today. The primitive folk style is nowhere more apparent than in the failed attempt at a *trompe à l'œil* apse on the front interior wall (below). The failure of the (original) artist to capture the correct perspective and depth merely adds to the already-great primitive charm. The hand-painted decorative band running around the walls provides visual unity to the interior paintings, but it is the treatment of the ceiling that not only surprises but stuns the unsuspecting visitor. One is reminded of the ceilings of the rococo-style churches of Upper Bavaria and Upper Austria. The intricacy of detail and the choice of colors are not merely surprising in a rural Georgia church, but amazing. The marbleized effect on the ceiling (lower photo, opposite). was obtained by holding (and moving) a lighted candle or oil-lamp flame close to the wet paint so that the black oil smoke adhered to the surface. The interior painting was beautifully restored by Biltmore, Campbell, Smith, Inc., of Asheville, North Carolina, circa 1983.

A Survey of Church Architecture in Rural Georgia

Kiokee Baptist Church (c. 1808) (Columbia County) was organized under the leadership of the intrepid Rev. Mr. Daniel Marshall in 1772 as Georgia's first Baptist congregation. Having endured persecution at the hands of the colonial authorities (see Introduction), the congregation prospered, making it today Georgia's oldest Baptist church. The very elegant masonry structure, of handmade bricks laid in Flemish bond, is the third to stand on this site and was completed in 1808. It stands beside the road in a clearing in the woods, inviting passers-by to visit the past. Kiokee Church is perhaps the best-preserved and least-altered of any ecclesiastical structure in Georgia, with the possible exception of Zion Episcopal Church in Talbotton, q.v. The interior is constructed entirely with wooden pegs. The building is beautifully maintained, but is used today only for special occasions, the congregation having built a newer, larger building for their use in nearby Appling, the county seat. Surely one of the most significant buildings in Georgia.

A Survey of Church Architecture in Rural Georgia

How Firm a Foundation

Episcopal Church of the Mediator (c. 1896), Washington (Wilkes County)

Practically nothing is known about the organization of the congregation or of the construction of this late-Victorian jewel. According to local legend, Robert Toombs, the "Unreconstructed Rebel," whose former home (now a museum) stands next door, donated the lot to the congregation for a building site so that the church building, once finished, would block his view of a detested neighbor. This tiny, sophisticated two-room church (see Introduction) is one of the most charming buildings in Georgia. The tower (with belfry) rises above the steep-pitched roof of the nave, and it contains the narthex, which is entered through the main entrance door. The native Georgia pine of the interior has attained a beautiful patina of age, making the church dark yet warm. One might almost call it cozy. Without a doubt, however, the main feature of this building is the stained glass, executed and installed in the mid-1960s, which is of international significance. The artist who executed the stained glass also executed the stained glass in the Cathedral of Saint John the Divine in New York City; in the Cathedral of Saint Vincent de Paul in Los Angeles; and in the Cathedral Church of Saints Peter and Paul in Washington, DC (also known as the

Washington or "National" Cathedral). The rich blue in these magnificent windows is today irreproducible, as the sand used in its manufacture is now too polluted for such use, making these windows all the more rare and significant. The five-panel lancet window in the rear wall of the nave (pg. 86) depicts Christ flanked by the traditional symbols of the four Evangelists. Along the left-hand side of the nave, the windows depict Old Testament personages. On the right-hand side are depicted the Lord's apostles, representative of the New Testament. The round window in the narthex (pg. 85) depicts St. Francis of Assisi ministering to the animals and is particularly charming.

Episcopal Church of the Mediator, Washington (Wilkes County) detail (Below). Looking up the nave towards the chancel and sanctuary. The burl-wood veneers on the front of the altar and on the bishop's chair are particularly fine.

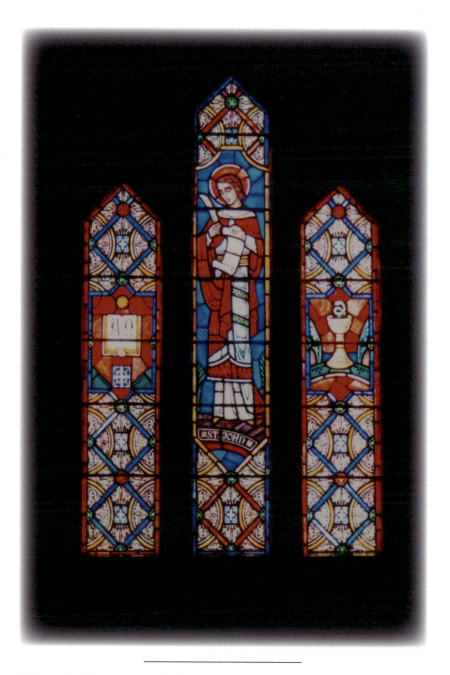

Episcopal Church of the Mediator (c. 1896), Washington-Wilkes. One of the magnificent internationally significant stained-glass lancet windows (c. 1965), this one depicting St. John the Evangelist.

A Survey of Church Architecture in Rural Georgia

How Firm a Foundation

A Survey of Church Architecture in Rural Georgia

Midway Congregational Church (c. 1792), Midway (Liberty County), replaces an earlier building (c. 1755) that had been torched by the British during the Revolution (two of Georgia's three Signers of the Declaration of Independence, Button Gwinnett and Lyman Hall, were members of this church). During the invasion of Georgia in 1864, Federal troops used the church as a slaughterhouse and the cemetery across the road to pen in the livestock. The soldiers used the church's melodian as a huge butcher-block. And when they moved on, they pushed the melodian down from the church's upstairs gallery, smashing it. Church members retrieved pieces of the shattered instrument and used them to build a small communion table, which is still in use. The frame clapboard building's main façade has five bays with two entrance doors below a closed gable punctuated by two ox-eye windows. The wood-shingled roof supports a small square tower that is topped by a balustrade and a small open spire. The two tiers of windows indicate the upstairs gallery that wraps around three of the building's interior walls. One of the most elegant and significant buildings in Georgia, and indeed, in the original thirteen states. A real must-see.

How Firm a Foundation

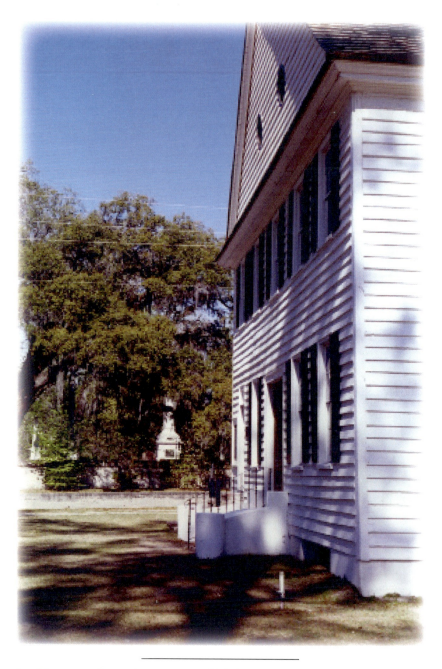

Looking past the main entrance of Midway Church towards the cemetery across the road.

Bibliography & Suggested Reading List

1. Blackburn, Joyce; *James Edward Oglethorpe,* JB Lippincott Co., Philadelphia & New York, 1970.

2. Brooks, Robert Preston; *History of Georgia,* Atkinson, Mentzer & Co., Atlanta, 1913.

3. Cashin, Edward J.; *Governor Henry Ellis and the Transformation of British North America,* University of Georgia Press, Athens, 1994.

4. Cofer, Loris D.; *Queensborough, the Irish Town and its Citizens,* May 1977, 2nd ed., 1990.

5. Coleman, Kenneth; *Georgia History in Outline,* University of Georgia Press, Athens, 1960.

6. Coleman, Kenneth, Gen. Ed.; Spalding, Boney, et al., authors, *A History of Georgia,* University of Georgia Press, Athens, 1977.

7. Crutchfield, James A.; *The Georgia Almanac and Book of Facts, 1989 – 1990,* Rutledge Hill Press, Nashville, 1988.

8. Davis, Harold E.; *The Fledgling Province: Social and Cultural Life in Colonial Georgia, 1733 – 1776,* University of North Carolina Press, Chapel Hill, 1976.

9. Diocese of Savannah; *A People of Faith: A Brief History of Catholicism in South Georgia,* Department of Christian Formation, Diocese of Savannah, undated (after 1978).

10. Evans, Lawton B.; *History of Georgia,* University Publishing Co., New York City & New Orleans, 1898.

11. Gardner, RG, et al.; *A History of the Georgia Baptist Association, 1784 – 1984,* Georgia Baptist Historical Society, Wilkes Publishing Co., Washington, Georgia, 1988.

12. Georgia Department of Natural Resources, *The Rock House, McDuffie County, Georgia, An Analysis of an Historic Site,* reprinted by the Wrightsborough Quaker Community Foundation, Inc.; with permission of Georgia DNR, 1977.

13. Lane, Mills; *The Architecture of the Old South: Georgia*, Beehive Press, Savannah, 1986.

14. Linley, John; *The Georgia Catalog: Historic American Buildings Survey*, University of Georgia Press, Athens, 1982.

15. McCain, James Ross; *Georgia as a Proprietary Province: The Execution of a Trust*, Richard G. Badger, Boston, 1917; Reprinted by the Reprint Co., Spartanburg, South Carolina, 1972.

16. Malone, HT; *The Episcopal Church in Georgia, 1733 – 1957,* The Protestant Episcopal Church in the Diocese of Atlanta, Foote & Davis, Athens, 1960.

17. Murray, Jane; *The Kings and Queens of England*, Charles Scribner's Sons, New York City, 1974.

18. Nichols, Frederick Doveton; *The Early Architecture of Georgia*, University of North Carolina Press, Chapel Hill, 1957.

19. Reese, TR; *Colonial Georgia: A Study in British Imperial Policy in the Eighteenth Century,* University of Georgia Press, Athens, 1963.

20. Riley, BF; *A History of the Baptists in the Southern States East of the Mississippi*, American Baptist Publication Society, Philadelphia, 1898.

21. Rubin, Rabbi Saul Jacob; *Third to None: The Saga of Savannah Jewry, 1733 – 1983*, Mickve Israel Congregation, Savannah, 1983.

22. Skeats, Walter W.; *The Etymological Dictionary of the English Language*, Oxford, England, The Clarendon Press, 1879, rev. ed., 1995.

23. Stevens, William Bacon; *A History of Georgia,* Beehive Press, Savannah, 1847, reprinted 1972.

24. Tauté, Anne, compiler; Brooke-Little, John, MSO, MA, FSA, Richmond Herald of Arms, editor; Pottinger, Don MA (HONS), DA, Unicorn Pursuivant of Arms, artist; *The Kings and Queens of Great Britain,* Elm Tree Press, London, 1976.

INDEX

A

Acadians 7, 8
Africa 66
Albemarle Sound 2
Altamaha River 2, 10, 23, 66
Altamirano, Archbishop 1
American bond 69
Americans With Disabilities Act 34
Anglicans 4, 6, 14, 26
Anne (ship) 5, 6
Argyle, duke of 3
Asbury, Bishop Francis 30, 90, 92
Asheville, North Carolina 78
Assisi, St. Francis of 83
Augsburg, Germany 18
Austria 18, 78
Austrians 19

B

Baltimore, Maryland 29, 31
Bamberg, Germany 21
Baptists 7, 9, 14, 26, 27, 29, 32-34, 50, 106
Barnwell, J.G. 54
Bavaria 78
Beaux Arts style 40, 94
Belgrade, siege of 3
Biltmore, Campbell, Smith, Inc. 78
Bloody Marsh, Battle of 10, 11
Board of Trade 2
Bolzius, Rev 15, 19-21
bond, American 69
bond, English 43, 94
bond, Flemish 80
Bray, Rev. Dr. Thomas 4, 8

C

Cajuns .... i, 7, 8
California 1, 107
Canada 7
Canterbury, Archbishop of 6

How Firm a Foundation

Carlisle, England 24
Caroline, Queen of England 15
Carthage 66
Cartlege, Constable Samuel 27, 28
Cashin, Prof. Dr. Edward 25, 105
Cathedral, "National" 83
Cathedral, Washington 83
Charles I, King of England 24
Charles II, King of England 2
Charleston, South Carolina 12
Churches:
    Abbey Church (Monastery of the Holy Spirit) 32, 41, 56
    Advent, Episcopal Church of the 41, 45, 46
    All Saints Episcopal 41, 54
    Bethabara Baptist 40, 42, 103
    Bethany Lutheran 18
    Bethel Presbyterian 10
    Bethesda Baptist 23, 30, 38, 39, 41, 69
    Christ Episcopal (Savannah Parish) 8, 14, 15, 18, 26
    Clarkesville Presbyterian 39
    Damascus Methodist 41, 77
    Ebenezer Presbyterian 10
    First Baptist (McRae, Georgia) 40
    Grace-Calvary Episcopal 36, 39, 41, 44, 73, 95
    Harvest Temple Church of God 39
    Hebron Presbyterian 41, 58
    Independent Presbyterian 11
    Jerusalem Lutheran 15, 18, 19, 36, 39, 41, 43, 44, 54, 73, 97
    Kiokee Baptist 27, 28, 38, 39, 41, 71, 80
    Liberty Methodist 29, 38, 39, 41, 90, 92
    Madison Presbyterian 41, 60, 62, 63
    Mediator, Episcopal Church of the 37, 41, 82-84
    Midway Congregational 12, 23, 24, 38, 39, 41, 50, 69, 87-89
    Old Emory Chapel 39, 41, 93
    Old Mercer Chapel 41, 50
    Old Stone 41, 55
    Piney Grove Missionary Baptist 41, 47
    Purification, Catholic Church of the 31, 42, 99, 101, 102
    Redeemer, Episcopal Church of the 41, 54
    Springfield Baptist 30
    St. Cyprian's Episcopal 41, 66, 68
    St. Mary's Presbyterian 39, 41, 64
    St. Michael's Episcopal 37, 40

St. Paul's Episcopal 16
Washington Presbyterian 12, 38, 39, 41, 52
Ways Baptist 39, 50
Zion Episcopal 37, 41, 44, 71-74, 76, 80, 97, 98
Coburg, Germany 21
Coleman, Professor Kenneth 5, 105
common bond 69
Concord, Massachusetts 28
Confederate States of America 31
Congregationalists 6, 12, 23, 25
Creek Nation 13
Cromwell, Oliver 16
Cuba 1, 10
Cumberland Island, Georgia 1
Cyprian, bishop & martyr 66

D

Deism 36
Disciples of Christ 32
Dorchester, Massachusetts 23
Dorchester, South Carolina 23
Duomo (Cathedral); Florence, Italy 71

E

East India Company 11
Ecclesiologist Magazine 71
Edinburgh (Scotland), Presbytery of 11
Edisto Island, South Carolina 11
Edward I, King of England 16
Edwards, Rev. Jonathan 36
Egmont, Earl of 4
Elliot, Rt. Rev. Stephen 71, 95
Ellis, Royal Governor of Georgia 25, 26, 105
Ellis Square (Savannah) 11
Emory University 41, 93
England 2-6, 8, 11, 15-17, 20, 23, 24, 28, 37, 66, 93, 106
England, Church of 4, 5, 8, 24, 25, 28, 37
England, Rev. Dr. 31
English bond 43, 94
Enlightenment, Age of 5, 35
Eugène of Savoy, Prince 3

F

Flemish bond. 80
Florence, Italy 71
Florida... i, 1, 2, 4, 10, 25
Foxe's Book of Martyrs (*Actes and Monuments*) 25
France..3, 12, 24, 25, 31, 35
Frankfurt-am-Main, Germany 21

G

George I, Elector of Hanover & King of England..........................24
George II, King of England 2, 15, 21
Georgia:
Cities & towns
    Appling 28, 80
    Atlanta..30, 56, 93, 94, 105, 106
    Augusta 13, 16, 27, 28, 30, 98, 107
    Bainbridge 40, 41, 94
    Clarkesville 39, 41, 44, 73, 95, 98
    Darien 10, 11, 23, 26, 41, 66, 68
    Frederica 15
    Greensboro 41, 54
    Griffin 39
    Locust Grove 31
    Louisville 10
    Lumpkin 77
    McRae..40
    Madison 41, 45, 46, 60, 62, 63
    Midway 12, 23, 24, 38, 39, 41, 50, 69, 87-89
    Milledgeville 37
    New Ebenezer 15, 18, 19
    Oxford 39, 41, 93
    Penfield 41, 50
    Queensborough 10, 105
    Quitman 40
    Ringgold 55
    Rome..54
    St. Mary's 39, 41, 64
    Savannah...............................i, 2, 6-9, 11, 12, 14, 15, 17, 18, 20-23,
                                                           6, 27, 30, 32, 94, 98, 105, 106
    Sharon 31, 42, 99
    Talbotton 37, 41, 44, 71-74, 76, 80, 97, 98
    Thomasville 41, 54
    Union Point 69

Vernonsburg 12
Vidette 10
Washington 12, 37-39, 41, 52, 53, 82-84, 105
Waynesboro 37, 40
Westville 41, 77
Wrightsborough 13, 29, 105
Counties
  Brooks 40
  Burke 10, 40
  Camden 39, 41, 64
  Catoosa 41, 55
  Columbia 27, 28, 38, 41, 71, 80
  Decatur 40, 41, 94
  Effingham 15, 18, 29, 30, 39, 41, 43, 44, 54, 73
  Franklin 41, 58
  Greene 23, 30, 38, 41, 50, 54, 69
  Habersham 39, 41, 73, 95
  Jefferson 10, 39, 50
  Liberty 12, 39, 41, 50, 69, 87
  McDuffie 13
  McIntosh 41, 66, 68
  Morgan 41, 45, 46, 60, 62, 63
  Oconee 40, 42, 103
  Richmond 29, 38, 41, 90
  Rockdale 32, 41, 56, 57
  Spalding 39
  Stewart 41, 77
  Talbot. 41, 71-73, 76
  Taliaferro 30, 31, 42, 99, 101
  Thomas 41, 47, 54
  Wilkes 12, 30, 37, 38, 41, 52, 53, 82-84
Georgia, Episcopal Diocese of 95
Georgia Historical Commission 64
Georgia, invasion of 11, 24, 60, 87
Georgia Salzburger Society 43
Germans 19, 22
Germany 18, 20, 21, 24, 32, 107
Gibson, Bishop 6
Glorious Revolution 3, 25
Godalming, Surrey, England 2
Gothic Revival style 37, 40, 45, 46, 71, 72
Gothic style 37, 56
Great Awakening 6, 27, 35, 38

111

Greek Revival style 50, 60, 95
Gronau, Rev. 19, 20
Guale 1, 2
Gunpowder Plot 25
Guy Fawkes 25
Gwinnett, Button 23, 87

H
Halifax Resolves 27
Hall, Dr. Lyman 23, 87
Herbert of Cherbury, Lord 8
Herbert, Rev. Dr. 8
Hereford (England) Cathedral 66
Highlanders, Scottish 10
Holy Spirit, Monastery of the 32, 41, 56, 57
Horse Creek Valley, South Carolina 27
Huguenots 10, 12, 23

I
Ireland 5, 6, 9, 24, 32
Irish 9, 10, 31, 32, 105

J
Jacobites 3, 24
Jacobite uprising .... i, 24
James Francis Edward, Prince 3, 24, 25
James I & VI, King of England & Scotland 24
James II & VII, King of England & Scotland 3, 25
James III & VIII, King of England & Scotland 3, 25
Jamestown, Virginia 25
Jews .... i, 6, 16, 17, 20, 21, 32
Johnson, Rev. Richard 71

K
Kassel, Germany 21
Keble, Rev. John 37
Kellogg, Ezra 95
Kentucky 56
Killian, Daniel 60

L
Lane, Mills 71

Leigh, Rev. James Wentworth 66
Lembke, Rev 19, 20
Lemoin, Father John 31
Lexington, Massachusetts 28
Little, Dr. Thomas..64
Locust Grove Academy 31
London, England...2, 9, 11, 12, 25, 106
Lords Proprietors 2
Los Angeles, California 82
Louisiana ....i, 8
Lutherans...6, 9, 13, 14, 17, 19, 21, 25, 32

M
Marshall, Mrs. Daniel 28
Marshall, Rev. Daniel ....i, 8, 27, 28, 80
Mary-Beatrice of Modena, Queen of England 25
Maryland 31
Marylanders..30
Mather, Rev. Cotton 36
Mather, Rev. Increase 36
McCain, Professor 8, 9, 106
McLeod, Rev. John 11
Medway River 23
Mercer, Rev. Jesse 50
Mercer University 41, 50
Methodist Church 29, 93
Methodists.. 9, 29, 30, 32-34
Miami County, Ohio 14
Mississippi River..25, 106
Mobile, Alabama 7, 25
Moravians..4, 13
Morehouse College 30

N
National Apostasy, The (sermon) 37
Netherlands, The...18, 21
New Amsterdam 17
New England 6, 17, 23, 36
New Mexico 1
New Orleans. 7, 25, 105
New York..17, 22, 82, 98, 105, 106
Newton, Sir Isaac 36
Norman-Irish 10

North Carolina 13, 27, 78, 105, 106
Nuñes, Dr. (physician) 16, 17

O
O'Brien, Father 31
Ogeechee River 10
Oglethorpe, Gen. Sir James Edward, baronet .... i, 2-6, 8, 10, 11
16-18, 22, 24, 105
Oglethorpe, Lady 3
Old Pretender 3, 24, 25
organ, Erben 98
organ, Pilcher 71, 75
Osgood, Rev. John 12, 23
Oxford Movement 37, 40, 97
Oxford (England), University of 3, 37, 106

P
Paris, France 3, 29
Paris, Treaty of 29
Parliament 3, 24, 25
Pennsylvania 13
Pensacola, Florida 7
Perceval, Viscount 4, 9
Philadelphia, Pennsylvania 66, 105, 106
Pietism 35
plain (vernacular) style 38, 99
Portugal, Grand Inquisitor of 16
Presbyterian Poplar, the 12, 53
Presbyterians 10-12, 14, 26, 32, 60
Provincial Assembly, Georgia 24
Puritans 23, 36

Q
Quakers 6, 9, 13, 29, 105
Queen Anne style 40

R
Rabenhorst, Rev. 19
Rationalism 35
Reformation 18, 35, 37, 38
Revolution, American 2, 7, 9, 12, 19, 22, 23
26, 28, 29, 33, 35, 43, 87, 89
Revolution, French 31, 35

Revolution, Industrial..35
Roman Catholics .... i, 1, 6, 7, 9, 17, 21, 22, 25
                                    29-32, 34, 42, 54, 99, 101, 102, 105
Rubin, Rabbi Saul...21, 22, 106

S
Sacred Harp (singing)..33
Salzburg, Austria...13, 18
Salzburgers.. 14, 15, 17-21, 43
Savannah, Catholic Diocese of 32, 105
Savannah River..2, 6, 18, 23, 27, 98
Scotch-Irish...10, 55
Scotland 11, 24
Scotland, Church of..11
Scots 11, 22, 23, 26
Screven, General...89
Shaftesbury, Lord 9
Society for the Promotion of Christian Knowledge 11
Society for the Propagation of the Gospel in Foreign Parts........4, 20
Sophia, Queen of England 24
South Carolina 11, 12, 23, 27, 29, 32, 71, 95, 106
Spain..1, 2, 11
Spalding, Professor 1, 105
Springer, Rev. John..12, 53
St. Andrew's Parish, Georgia...26
St. Augustine, Florida 1, 2, 7
St. Catherine's Island, Georgia 1
Ste.-Geneviève, Missouri 25
St. George's Parish, Georgia..10
St.-Germain, France 3
St. John's Parish, Georgia 23
St. John the Divine, Cathedral of 82
St. John the Evangelist (window) 84
St. Paul's Parish, Georgia 27
Ss. Peter & Paul, Cathedral Church of 82
St. Simon's Island, Georgia 15
St. Vincent de Paul, Cathedral of 82
Stephens, Alexander Hamilton 31
Stevens, Professor...6, 11, 106
Stuart, House of 3, 24
Sujet, Father..31
Surrey, England 2

Synagogues:
- Ahavath Achim, Atlanta 94
- Jeshuat Israel (Touro), Rhode Island 22
- Shearith Israel, New York 21
- Temple Bethel; Bainbridge, Georgia 40, 41, 94
- TheTemple ; Atlanta, Georgia 94
- Touro (Jeshuat Israel), Rhode Island 22

T
Tennessee 55
Texas 1
Toombs, Robert 82
Tractarians 37
Trappist Order 56
Treutlen, John Adam, Gov. of Georgia 19
Trustees of the Georgia colony 2, 4-6, 8, 9, 12, 14-18, 23

U
Unitarianism 36

V
van Buren, Jarvis 95
van Buren, President Martin 95
vernacular (plain) style 38, 39, 45, 50, 52, 54, 69, 90, 95, 99
Virginia 12, 25, 27
Voltaire 36

W
War Between the States 43
Washington, D.C. 82, 83
Wesley, Rev. Charles 93
Wesley, Rev. John .... i, 7, 8, 13, 14, 36, 93
Wesleys, the 6, 37
Westbrook Place 2
Whitefield, Rev. George 5, 6, 36
William & Mary, king & queen of England 3
William of Orange, Prince 3, 25
Winchester, Virginia 27
Windsor, Connecticut 27
Würzburg, Germany 21

Z
Zouberbuehler, Rev. Bartholomew 5, 9
Zubly, Rev. J. J. 9, 12

About the Author

Richard Noegel is a native of Augusta, Georgia. He is a graduate of Richmond Academy (Augusta), of the University of Georgia (Athens), of the Defense Language Institute (Monterey, California), and of the Goethe Institut in Munich, Germany, where he also taught English as a foreign language. He is retired from the Centers for Disease Control & Prevention (CDC), where he was a medical writer and editor. Richard is a long-time student of history, with a particular interest in Georgia history. He is the father of two and the grandfather of three. He lives in Augusta.

About the Photographer

Carol J. Mohor was born in New Jersey, and she considers herself at home when she is at "the Jersey Shore." She has loved art and photography since she was a child.

She entered the University of Georgia as a Photographic Design major in 1974. It was during her college years that she felt called to teach the subject she loves most—art—and she added education as part of her degree program. She taught art in the public schools of Georgia for more than 30 years.

Now retired, Carol has never stopped taking "artistic" photographs, and she continually strives to succeed professionally in photography. This book has proven to be a major part of that goal. She currently resides in McDonough, Georgia. Carol enjoys playing the guitar, singing in church, and waiting to see how her first published collection of photographs is received.

CPSIA information can be obtained
at www.ICGtesting.com
Printed in the USA
LVIC06n0735100814
398397LV00012B/69

Entrance to Midway Church cemetery, burial place of Revolutionary War General Screven.

How Firm a Foundation

Liberty Methodist Church in Hephzibah (Richmond County) was built circa 1804 as the home of Georgia's first and oldest Methodist congregation (c. 1783–85). This simple frame structure is the archetype of the vernacular one-room meeting-house style in Georgia, with three bays on the sides and two bays on each end beneath open gables. The sixteen-over-sixteen windows fill the interior with light and grant a view of the pretty, pastoral cemetery. The perboards that served to separate the women's and children's seating area from that of the men are still intact and in place (opposite). The pulpit is still in use today at which Bishop Francis Asbury preached when he visited the congregation in 1790. The building was abandoned in the 1960s, but was reclaimed and beautifully restored and sensitively modernized circa 1979–81.

A Survey of Church Architecture in Rural Georgia

How Firm a Foundation

The pulpit at which Bishop Asbury preached at Liberty Church in 1790.

A Survey of Church Architecture in Rural Georgia

Atlanta's Emory University was born here in Oxford (Newton County) in December 1836 as Emory College when the Methodist Church expanded its efforts in the field of education in Georgia. Oxford, chartered in December 1839, was named for Oxford, England, that great seat of learning from which both John and Charles Wesley had been graduated. The "Old Church," seen here, was built in 1841, with the wings being added in 1878. Emory's first commencement exercises were held here in 1843.

How Firm a Foundation

Temple Bethel (c. 1920) in Bainbridge (Decatur County) is a perfectly proportioned masonry structure. It calls to mind the Old Testament text: "Strength and beauty are in His sanctuary." Surely, Temple Bethel expresses both of those qualities. The bricks are laid in English bond (except for those below the water table and those right above the cornice board). Particularly noteworthy is the use of the beautiful Ionic columns *in antis* to create a recessed porch. This small building's proportions and its Neoclassical Revival and Beaux Arts elements make it one of the loveliest Jewish houses of worship anywhere in Georgia, urban or rural. As such, it may be compared favorably with the exquisite Ahavath Achim Synagogue or with the dignified classical-style Temple, both in Atlanta, or with the magnificent Mickve Israel synagogue in Savannah.

Grace-Calvary Episcopal Church (c. 1842) in Clarkesville (Habersham County) was built for a congregation (Grace Church) that had been established by a missionary priest, Ezra Kellogg, in his home in Clarkesville in 1838. Clarkesville, founded 1823, had quickly become a summer resort for residents of lower-lying, hotter areas of Georgia and South Carolina, and it was they who constituted Grace Church. Construction on this building was begun in 1839 under the supervision of Jarvis van Buren, a relative of U.S. President Martin van Buren. (Grace Church was merged with Calvary Church, a nearby congregation, in 1972, hence the present name).

(NEXT PAGE) In May 1840, the Episcopal Diocese of Georgia, in convention in Clarkesville (in the Methodist Church), elected Stephen Elliot the first Bishop of Georgia. It was the Right Reverend Mr. Elliot who consecrated the newly completed Grace Church structure on October 10, 1842. The charming white frame building is a vernacular expression of the Greek Revival style, which was beginning to gain widespread popularity in America at that time. The original hand-blown glass still glazes the enormous 42-over-42 windows, with their delicate muntins.

How Firm a Foundation

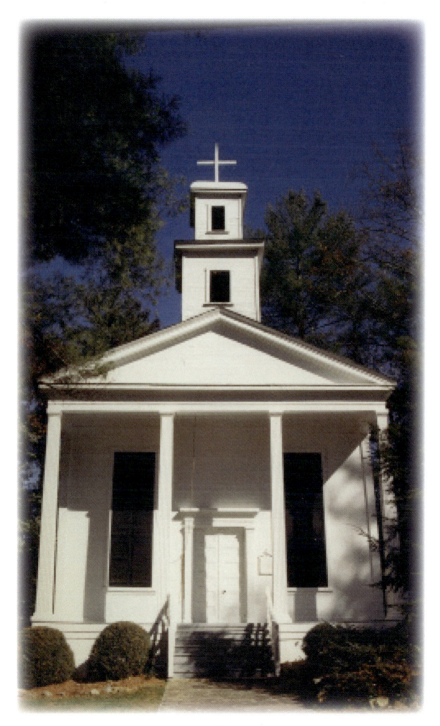

A Survey of Church Architecture in Rural Georgia

The central arrangement of the pulpit with the Holy Table expresses the practices of pre-Oxford Movement Anglicanism (see Introduction; cf. Jerusalem Lutheran Church). The most distinctive feature of the building's interior is probably the box pews which served in former times as a stop to drafts during cold weather (cf. Zion Episcopal Church, Talbotton). Rental of box pews also provided income to the church.

The Erben organ, commissioned in 1848 by a group of ladies within the congregation, was installed in 1852. Still in regular use today, it is one of the oldest working pipe organs in Georgia (cf. Zion Church, Talbotton). It was built at the Erben factory in New York, disassembled and sent by ship to Savannah, taken up the Savannah River to Augusta by steamboat, then overland by ox-drawn wagon to Clarkesville. It stands in the former slave gallery at the rear of the church. The black walnut instrument still boasts its original finish. The one-manual tracker-action organ retains the Baroque-period quality of sound found in earlier European instruments. It was electrified in 1972.

Roman Catholic Church of the Purification (c. 1883), Sharon (Taliaferro County). This vernacular- or plain-style clapboard building is home to Georgia's first and oldest Catholic congregation and cemetery. Dedicated to the feast of the Purification of the Blessed Virgin Mary (2 February), the atmosphere both within the building and without is one of repose. The heart of pine floors have aged to a rich brown with a beautiful reddish tint.

The refined and extraordinarily substantial pews were built to last at least until the Day of Judgment.

Catholic Church of the Purification (c. 1883) Taliaferro County. The rich brown and the beautiful open grain of fine Honduras mahogany beautify the holy water stoup near the entrance.

Catholic Church of the Purification (c. 1883). The lovely altar and tabernacle.

A Survey of Church Architecture in Rural Georgia

Bethabara Baptist Church (c. 1910) in Oconee County is a beautiful, early 20th-century masonry structure with several interesting features. Note the false dome (partially obscured by the tree), which is not visible inside. The church's interior is beautified with brilliant 20th-century stained glass and  magnificent English-made walnut pews. The ceiling retains its original pressed-tin decoration. Worth a visit. Ask to see the floor joists.

Bethabara Baptist Church (c. 1910) stained glass depiction of John the Baptist baptizing Jesus Christ.